AFRIKAANS
VOCABULARY

ENGLISH-AFRIKAANS

The most useful words
To expand your lexicon and sharpen
your language skills

7000 words

Afrikaans vocabulary for English speakers - 7000 words

By Andrey Taranov

T&P Books vocabularies are intended for helping you learn, memorize and review foreign words. The dictionary is divided into themes, covering all major spheres of everyday activities, business, science, culture, etc.

The process of learning words using T&P Books' theme-based dictionaries gives you the following advantages:

- Correctly grouped source information predetermines success at subsequent stages of word memorization
- Availability of words derived from the same root allowing memorization of word units (rather than separate words)
- Small units of words facilitate the process of establishing associative links needed for consolidation of vocabulary
- Level of language knowledge can be estimated by the number of learned words

T&P Books Publishing
www.tpbooks.com

ISBN: 978-1-78716-484-0

This book is also available in E-book formats.
Please visit www.tpbooks.com or the major online bookstores.

AFRIKAANS VOCABULARY
for English speakers

T&P Books vocabularies are intended to help you learn, memorize, and review foreign words. The vocabulary contains over 7000 commonly used words arranged thematically.

- Vocabulary contains the most commonly used words
- Recommended as an addition to any language course
- Meets the needs of beginners and advanced learners of foreign languages
- Convenient for daily use, revision sessions, and self-testing activities
- Allows you to assess your vocabulary

Special features of the vocabulary

- Words are organized according to their meaning, not alphabetically
- Words are presented in three columns to facilitate the reviewing and self-testing processes
- Words in groups are divided into small blocks to facilitate the learning process
- The vocabulary offers a convenient and simple transcription of each foreign word

The vocabulary has 198 topics including:

Basic Concepts, Numbers, Colors, Months, Seasons, Units of Measurement, Clothing & Accessories, Food & Nutrition, Restaurant, Family Members, Relatives, Character, Feelings, Emotions, Diseases, City, Town, Sightseeing, Shopping, Money, House, Home, Office, Working in the Office, Import & Export, Marketing, Job Search, Sports, Education, Computer, Internet, Tools, Nature, Countries, Nationalities and more ...

T&P BOOKS' THEME-BASED DICTIONARIES

The Correct System for Memorizing Foreign Words

Acquiring vocabulary is one of the most important elements of learning a foreign language, because words allow us to express our thoughts, ask questions, and provide answers. An inadequate vocabulary can impede communication with a foreigner and make it difficult to understand a book or movie well.

The pace of activity in all spheres of modern life, including the learning of modern languages, has increased. Today, we need to memorize large amounts of information (grammar rules, foreign words, etc.) within a short period. However, this does not need to be difficult. All you need to do is to choose the right training materials, learn a few special techniques, and develop your individual training system.

Having a system is critical to the process of language learning. Many people fail to succeed in this regard; they cannot master a foreign language because they fail to follow a system comprised of selecting materials, organizing lessons, arranging new words to be learned, and so on. The lack of a system causes confusion and eventually, lowers self-confidence.

T&P Books' theme-based dictionaries can be included in the list of elements needed for creating an effective system for learning foreign words. These dictionaries were specially developed for learning purposes and are meant to help students effectively memorize words and expand their vocabulary.

Generally speaking, the process of learning words consists of three main elements:

- Reception (creation or acquisition) of a training material, such as a word list
- Work aimed at memorizing new words
- Work aimed at reviewing the learned words, such as self-testing

All three elements are equally important since they determine the quality of work and the final result. All three processes require certain skills and a well-thought-out approach.

New words are often encountered quite randomly when learning a foreign language and it may be difficult to include them all in a unified list. As a result, these words remain written on scraps of paper, in book margins, textbooks, and so on. In order to systematize such words, we have to create and continually update a "book of new words." A paper notebook, a netbook, or a tablet PC can be used for these purposes.

This "book of new words" will be your personal, unique list of words. However, it will only contain the words that you came across during the learning process. For example, you might have written down the words "Sunday," "Tuesday," and "Friday." However, there are additional words for days of the week, for example, "Saturday," that are missing, and your list of words would be incomplete. Using a theme dictionary, in addition to the "book of new words," is a reasonable solution to this problem.

The theme-based dictionary may serve as the basis for expanding your vocabulary.

It will be your big "book of new words" containing the most frequently used words of a foreign language already included. There are quite a few theme-based dictionaries available, and you should ensure that you make the right choice in order to get the maximum benefit from your purchase.

Therefore, we suggest using theme-based dictionaries from T&P Books Publishing as an aid to learning foreign words. Our books are specially developed for effective use in the sphere of vocabulary systematization, expansion and review.

Theme-based dictionaries are not a magical solution to learning new words. However, they can serve as your main database to aid foreign-language acquisition. Apart from theme dictionaries, you can have copybooks for writing down new words, flash cards, glossaries for various texts, as well as other resources; however, a good theme dictionary will always remain your primary collection of words.

T&P Books' theme-based dictionaries are specialty books that contain the most frequently used words in a language.

The main characteristic of such dictionaries is the division of words into themes. For example, the *City* theme contains the words "street," "crossroads," "square," "fountain," and so on. The *Talking* theme might contain words like "to talk," "to ask," "question," and "answer".

All the words in a theme are divided into smaller units, each comprising 3–5 words. Such an arrangement improves the perception of words and makes the learning process less tiresome. Each unit contains a selection of words with similar meanings or identical roots. This allows you to learn words in small groups and establish other associative links that have a positive effect on memorization.

The words on each page are placed in three columns: a word in your native language, its translation, and its transcription. Such positioning allows for the use of techniques for effective memorization. After closing the translation column, you can flip through and review foreign words, and vice versa. "This is an easy and convenient method of review – one that we recommend you do often."

Our theme-based dictionaries contain transcriptions for all the foreign words. Unfortunately, none of the existing transcriptions are able to convey the exact nuances of foreign pronunciation. That is why we recommend using the transcriptions only as a supplementary learning aid. Correct pronunciation can only be acquired with the help of sound. Therefore our collection includes audio theme-based dictionaries.

The process of learning words using T&P Books' theme-based dictionaries gives you the following advantages:

- You have correctly grouped source information, which predetermines your success at subsequent stages of word memorization
- Availability of words derived from the same root (lazy, lazily, lazybones), allowing you to memorize word units instead of separate words
- Small units of words facilitate the process of establishing associative links needed for consolidation of vocabulary
- You can estimate the number of learned words and hence your level of language knowledge
- The dictionary allows for the creation of an effective and high-quality revision process
- You can revise certain themes several times, modifying the revision methods and techniques
- Audio versions of the dictionaries help you to work out the pronunciation of words and develop your skills of auditory word perception

The T&P Books' theme-based dictionaries are offered in several variants differing in the number of words: 1.500, 3.000, 5.000, 7.000, and 9.000 words. There are also dictionaries containing 15,000 words for some language combinations. Your choice of dictionary will depend on your knowledge level and goals.

We sincerely believe that our dictionaries will become your trusty assistant in learning foreign languages and will allow you to easily acquire the necessary vocabulary.

TABLE OF CONTENTS

PRONUNCIATION GUIDE

T&P phonetic alphabet	Afrikaans example	English example
[a]	land	shorter than in ask
[ã]	straat	calf, palm
[æ]	hout	chess, man
[o], [ɔ]	Australië	drop, baught
[e]	metaal	elm, medal
[ɛ]	aanlê	man, bad
[ə]	filter	driver, teacher
[ɪ]	uur	big, America
[i]	billik	shorter than in feet
[ĩ]	naïef	tree, big
[o]	koppie	pod, John
[ø]	akteur	eternal, church
[œ]	fluit	German Hölle
[u]	hulle	book
[ʊ]	hout	good, booklet
[b]	bakker	baby, book
[d]	donder	day, doctor
[f]	navraag	face, food
[g]	burger	game, gold
[h]	driehoek	home, have
[j]	byvoeg	yes, New York
[k]	kamera	clock, kiss
[l]	loon	lace, people
[m]	môre	magic, milk
[n]	neef	sang, thing
[p]	pyp	pencil, private
[r]	rigting	rice, radio
[s]	oplos	city, boss
[t]	lood, tenk	tourist, trip
[v]	bewaar	very, river
[w]	oorwinnaar	vase, winter
[z]	zoem	zebra, please
[dʒ]	enjin	joke, general
[ʃ]	artisjok	machine, shark
[ŋ]	kans	English, ring

T&P phonetic alphabet	Afrikaans example	English example
[tʃ]	tjek	church, French
[ʒ]	beige	forge, pleasure
[x]	agent	as in Scots 'loch'

ABBREVIATIONS
used in the vocabulary

English abbreviations

ab.	-	about
adj	-	adjective
adv	-	adverb
anim.	-	animate
as adj	-	attributive noun used as adjective
e.g.	-	for example
etc.	-	et cetera
fam.	-	familiar
fem.	-	feminine
form.	-	formal
inanim.	-	inanimate
masc.	-	masculine
math	-	mathematics
mil.	-	military
n	-	noun
pl	-	plural
pron.	-	pronoun
sb	-	somebody
sing.	-	singular
sth	-	something
v aux	-	auxiliary verb
vi	-	intransitive verb
vi, vt	-	intransitive, transitive verb
vt	-	transitive verb

BASIC CONCEPTS

Basic concepts. Part 1

1. Pronouns

I, me	ek, my	[ɛk], [maj]
you	jy	[jaj]
he	hy	[haj]
she	sy	[saj]
it	dit	[dit]
we	ons	[ɔŋs]
you (to a group)	julle	[julːə]
you (polite, sing.)	u	[u]
you (polite, pl)	u	[u]
they	hulle	[hulːə]

2. Greetings. Salutations. Farewells

Hello! (fam.)	Hallo!	[hallo!]
Hello! (form.)	Hallo!	[hallo!]
Good morning!	Goeie môre!	[χuje mɔrə!]
Good afternoon!	Goeiemiddag!	[χuje·middaχ!]
Good evening!	Goeienaand!	[χuje·nãnt!]
to say hello	dagsê	[daχsɛ:]
Hi! (hello)	Hallo!	[hallo!]
greeting (n)	groet	[χrut]
to greet (vt)	groet	[χrut]
How are you?	Hoe gaan dit?	[hu χãn dit?]
What's new?	Hoe gaan dit?	[hu χãn dit?]
Goodbye!	Totsiens!	[totsiŋs!]
Bye!	Koebaai!	[kubãi!]
See you soon!	Totsiens!	[totsiŋs!]
Farewell!	Totsiens!	[totsiŋs!]
Farewell! (to a friend)	Mooi loop!	[moj loep!]
Farewell! (form.)	Vaarwel!	[fãrwel!]
to say goodbye	afskeid neem	[afskæjt neəm]
So long!	Koebaai!	[kubãi!]
Thank you!	Dankie!	[danki!]

Thank you very much!	Baie dankie!	[baje danki!]
You're welcome	Plesier	[plesir]
Don't mention it!	Plesier!	[plesir!]
It was nothing	Plesier	[plesir]

Excuse me! (fam.)	Ekskuus!	[ɛkskɪs!]
Excuse me! (form.)	Verskoon my!	[ferskoən maj!]
to excuse (forgive)	verskoon	[ferskoən]

to apologize (vi)	verskoning vra	[ferskoniŋ fra]
My apologies	Verskoning	[ferskoniŋ]
I'm sorry!	Ek is jammer!	[ɛk is jammər!]
to forgive (vt)	vergewe	[ferχevə]
It's okay! (that's all right)	Maak nie saak nie!	[māk ni sāk ni!]
please (adv)	asseblief	[asseblif]

Don't forget!	Vergeet dit nie!	[ferχeət dit ni!]
Certainly!	Beslis!	[beslis!]
Of course not!	Natuurlik nie!	[natɪrlik ni!]
Okay! (I agree)	OK!	[okej!]
That's enough!	Dis genoeg!	[dis χenuχ!]

3. Cardinal numbers. Part 1

0 zero	nul	[nul]
1 one	een	[eən]
2 two	twee	[tweə]
3 three	drie	[dri]
4 four	vier	[fir]

5 five	vyf	[fajf]
6 six	ses	[ses]
7 seven	sewe	[sevə]
8 eight	ag	[aχ]
9 nine	nege	[neχə]

10 ten	tien	[tin]
11 eleven	elf	[ɛlf]
12 twelve	twaalf	[twālf]
13 thirteen	dertien	[dertin]
14 fourteen	veertien	[feərtin]

15 fifteen	vyftien	[fajftin]
16 sixteen	sestien	[sestin]
17 seventeen	sewetien	[sevətin]
18 eighteen	agtien	[aχtin]
19 nineteen	negetien	[neχetin]

| 20 twenty | twintig | [twintəχ] |
| 21 twenty-one | een-en-twintig | [eən-en-twintəχ] |

| 22 twenty-two | **twee-en-twintig** | [tweə-en-twintəχ] |
| 23 twenty-three | **drie-en-twintig** | [dri-en-twintəχ] |

30 thirty	**dertig**	[dertəχ]
31 thirty-one	**een-en-dertig**	[eən-en-dertəχ]
32 thirty-two	**twee-en-dertig**	[tweə-en-dertəχ]
33 thirty-three	**drie-en-dertig**	[dri-en-dertəχ]

40 forty	**veertig**	[feərtəχ]
41 forty-one	**een-en-veertig**	[eən-en-feərtəχ]
42 forty-two	**twee-en-veertig**	[tweə-en-feərtəχ]
43 forty-three	**vier-en-veertig**	[fir-en-feərtəχ]

50 fifty	**vyftig**	[fajftəχ]
51 fifty-one	**een-en-vyftig**	[eən-en-fajftəχ]
52 fifty-two	**twee-en-vyftig**	[tweə-en-fajftəχ]
53 fifty-three	**drie-en-vyftig**	[dri-en-fajftəχ]

60 sixty	**sestig**	[sestəχ]
61 sixty-one	**een-en-sestig**	[eən-en-sestəχ]
62 sixty-two	**twee-en-sestig**	[tweə-en-sestəχ]
63 sixty-three	**drie-en-sestig**	[dri-en-sestəχ]

70 seventy	**sewentig**	[seventəχ]
71 seventy-one	**een-en-sewentig**	[eən-en-seventəχ]
72 seventy-two	**twee-en-sewentig**	[tweə-en-seventəχ]
73 seventy-three	**drie-en-sewentig**	[dri-en-seventəχ]

80 eighty	**tagtig**	[taχtəχ]
81 eighty-one	**een-en-tagtig**	[eən-en-taχtəχ]
82 eighty-two	**twee-en-tagtig**	[tweə-en-taχtəχ]
83 eighty-three	**drie-en-tagtig**	[dri-en-taχtəχ]

90 ninety	**negentig**	[neχentəχ]
91 ninety-one	**een-en-negentig**	[eən-en-neχentəχ]
92 ninety-two	**twee-en-negentig**	[tweə-en-neχentəχ]
93 ninety-three	**drie-en-negentig**	[dri-en-neχentəχ]

4. Cardinal numbers. Part 2

100 one hundred	**honderd**	[hondərt]
200 two hundred	**tweehonderd**	[tweə·hondərt]
300 three hundred	**driehonderd**	[dri·hondərt]
400 four hundred	**vierhonderd**	[fir·hondərt]
500 five hundred	**vyfhonderd**	[fajf·hondərt]

600 six hundred	**seshonderd**	[ses·hondərt]
700 seven hundred	**sewehonderd**	[sevə·hondərt]
800 eight hundred	**aghonderd**	[aχ·hondərt]
900 nine hundred	**negehonderd**	[neχə·hondərt]

1000 one thousand	**duisend**	[dœisent]
2000 two thousand	**tweeduisend**	[twee·dœisent]
3000 three thousand	**drieduisend**	[dri·dœisent]
10000 ten thousand	**tienduisend**	[tin·dœisent]
one hundred thousand	**honderdduisend**	[hondərt·dajsent]
million	**miljoen**	[miljun]
billion	**miljard**	[miljart]

5. Numbers. Fractions

fraction	**breuk**	[brøək]
one half	**helfte**	[hɛlftə]
one third	**derde**	[derdə]
one quarter	**kwart**	[kwart]
one eighth	**agste**	[aχstə]
one tenth	**tiende**	[tində]
two thirds	**twee derde**	[twee derdə]
three quarters	**driekwart**	[drikwart]

6. Numbers. Basic operations

subtraction	**aftrekking**	[aftrɛkkiŋ]
to subtract (vi, vt)	**aftrek**	[aftrek]
division	**deling**	[deliŋ]
to divide (vt)	**deel**	[deəl]
addition	**optelling**	[optɛlliŋ]
to add up (vt)	**optel**	[optəl]
to add (vi, vt)	**optel**	[optəl]
multiplication	**vermenigvuldiging**	[fermeniχ·fuldəχiŋ]
to multiply (vt)	**vermenigvuldig**	[fermeniχ·fuldəχ]

7. Numbers. Miscellaneous

digit, figure	**syfer**	[sajfər]
number	**nommer**	[nommər]
numeral	**telwoord**	[tɛlwoərt]
minus sign	**minusteken**	[minus·tekən]
plus sign	**plusteken**	[plus·tekən]
formula	**formule**	[formulə]
calculation	**berekening**	[berekeniŋ]
to count (vi, vt)	**tel**	[təl]
to count up	**optel**	[optəl]
to compare (vt)	**vergelyk**	[ferχəlajk]

| How much? | Hoeveel? | [hufeəl?] |
| How many? | Hoeveel? | [hufeəl?] |

sum, total	som, totaal	[som], [totāl]
result	resultaat	[resultāt]
remainder	oorskot	[oərskot]

little (I had ~ time)	min	[min]
few (I have ~ friends)	min	[min]
the rest	die res	[di res]
dozen	dosyn	[dosajn]

in half (adv)	middeldeur	[middəldøər]
equally (evenly)	gelyk	[χelajk]
half	helfte	[hɛlftə]
time (three ~s)	maal	[māl]

8. The most important verbs. Part 1

to advise (vt)	aanraai	[ānrāi]
to agree (say yes)	saamstem	[sāmstem]
to answer (vi, vt)	antwoord	[antwoərt]
to apologize (vi)	verskoning vra	[ferskoniŋ fra]
to arrive (vi)	aankom	[ānkom]

to ask (~ oneself)	vra	[fra]
to ask (~ sb to do sth)	vra	[fra]
to be (vi)	wees	[veəs]

to be afraid	bang wees	[baŋ veəs]
to be hungry	honger wees	[hoŋər veəs]
to be interested in ...	belangstel in ...	[belaŋstəl in ...]
to be needed	nodig wees	[nodəχ veəs]
to be surprised	verbaas wees	[ferbās veəs]

to be thirsty	dors wees	[dors veəs]
to begin (vt)	begin	[beχin]
to belong to ...	behoort aan ...	[behoərt ān ...]
to boast (vi)	spog	[spoχ]
to break (split into pieces)	breek	[breək]

to call (~ for help)	roep	[rup]
can (v aux)	kan	[kan]
to catch (vt)	vang	[faŋ]
to change (vt)	verander	[ferandər]
to choose (select)	kies	[kis]

to come down (the stairs)	afkom	[afkom]
to compare (vt)	vergelyk	[ferχəlajk]
to complain (vi, vt)	kla	[kla]

to confuse (mix up)	verwar	[ferwar]
to continue (vt)	aangaan	[ānχān]
to control (vt)	kontroleer	[kontroleər]
to cook (dinner)	kook	[koək]
to cost (vt)	kos	[kos]
to count (add up)	tel	[təl]
to count on ...	reken op ...	[reken op ...]
to create (vt)	skep	[skep]
to cry (weep)	huil	[hœil]

9. The most important verbs. Part 2

to deceive (vi, vt)	bedrieg	[bedrəχ]
to decorate (tree, street)	versier	[fersir]
to defend (a country, etc.)	verdedig	[ferdedəχ]
to demand (request firmly)	eis	[æjs]
to dig (vt)	grawe	[χravə]
to discuss (vt)	bespreek	[bespreək]
to do (vt)	doen	[dun]
to doubt (have doubts)	twyfel	[twajfəl]
to drop (let fall)	laat val	[lāt fal]
to enter (room, house, etc.)	binnegaan	[binnəχān]
to excuse (forgive)	verskoon	[ferskoən]
to exist (vi)	bestaan	[bestān]
to expect (foresee)	voorsien	[foərsin]
to explain (vt)	verduidelik	[ferdœidəlik]
to fall (vi)	val	[fal]
to find (vt)	vind	[fint]
to finish (vt)	klaarmaak	[klārmāk]
to fly (vi)	vlieg	[fliχ]
to follow ... (come after)	volg ...	[folχ ...]
to forget (vi, vt)	vergeet	[ferχeət]
to forgive (vt)	vergewe	[ferχevə]
to give (vt)	gee	[χeə]
to go (on foot)	gaan	[χān]
to go for a swim	gaan swem	[χān swem]
to go out (for dinner, etc.)	uitgaan	[œitχān]
to guess (the answer)	raai	[rāi]
to have (vt)	hê	[hɛː]
to have breakfast	ontbyt	[ontbajt]
to have dinner	aandete gebruik	[āndetə χebrœik]
to have lunch	gaan eet	[χān eət]

to hear (vt)	hoor	[hoər]
to help (vt)	help	[hɛlp]
to hide (vt)	wegsteek	[veχsteək]
to hope (vi, vt)	hoop	[hoəp]
to hunt (vi, vt)	jag	[jaχ]
to hurry (vi)	opskud	[opskut]

10. The most important verbs. Part 3

to inform (vt)	in kennis stel	[in kɛnnis stəl]
to insist (vi, vt)	aandring	[āndriŋ]
to insult (vt)	beledig	[beledəχ]
to invite (vt)	uitnooi	[œitnoj]
to joke (vi)	grappies maak	[χrappis māk]

to keep (vt)	bewaar	[bevār]
to keep silent	stilbly	[stilblaj]
to kill (vt)	doodmaak	[doədmāk]
to know (sb)	ken	[ken]
to know (sth)	weet	[veət]
to laugh (vi)	lag	[laχ]

to liberate (city, etc.)	bevry	[befraj]
to like (I like …)	hou van	[hæʊ fan]
to look for … (search)	soek …	[suk …]
to love (sb)	liefhê	[lifhɛ:]

to manage, to run	beheer	[beheər]
to mean (signify)	beteken	[betekən]
to mention (talk about)	verwys na	[ferwajs na]
to miss (school, etc.)	bank	[bank]
to notice (see)	raaksien	[rāksin]

to object (vi, vt)	beswaar maak	[beswār māk]
to observe (see)	waarneem	[vārneəm]
to open (vt)	oopmaak	[oəpmāk]
to order (meal, etc.)	bestel	[bestəl]
to order (mil.)	beveel	[befeəl]
to own (possess)	besit	[besit]

to participate (vi)	deelneem	[deəlneəm]
to pay (vi, vt)	betaal	[betāl]
to permit (vt)	toestaan	[tustān]
to plan (vt)	beplan	[beplan]
to play (children)	speel	[speəl]

to pray (vi, vt)	bid	[bit]
to prefer (vt)	verkies	[ferkis]
to promise (vt)	beloof	[beloəf]
to pronounce (vt)	uitspreek	[œitspreək]

to propose (vt)	voorstel	[foərstəl]
to punish (vt)	straf	[straf]

11. The most important verbs. Part 4

to read (vi, vt)	lees	[leəs]
to recommend (vt)	aanbeveel	[ānbefeəl]
to refuse (vi, vt)	weier	[væejer]
to regret (be sorry)	jammer wees	[jammər veəs]
to rent (sth from sb)	huur	[hɪr]

to repeat (say again)	herhaal	[herhāl]
to reserve, to book	bespreek	[bespreək]
to run (vi)	hardloop	[hardloəp]
to save (rescue)	red	[ret]
to say (~ thank you)	sê	[sɛ:]

to scold (vt)	uitvaar teen	[œitfār teən]
to see (vt)	sien	[sin]
to sell (vt)	verkoop	[ferkoəp]
to send (vt)	stuur	[stɪr]
to shoot (vi)	skiet	[skit]

to shout (vi)	skreeu	[skriʊ]
to show (vt)	wys	[vajs]
to sign (document)	teken	[tekən]
to sit down (vi)	gaan sit	[χān sit]

to smile (vi)	glimlag	[χlimlaχ]
to speak (vi, vt)	praat	[prāt]
to steal (money, etc.)	steel	[steəl]
to stop (for pause, etc.)	stilhou	[stilhæʊ]
to stop (please ~ calling me)	ophou	[ophæʊ]

to study (vt)	studeer	[studeər]
to swim (vi)	swem	[swem]
to take (vt)	vat	[fat]
to think (vi, vt)	dink	[dink]
to threaten (vt)	dreig	[dræjχ]

to touch (with hands)	aanraak	[ānrāk]
to translate (vt)	vertaal	[fertāl]
to trust (vt)	vertrou	[fertræʊ]
to try (attempt)	probeer	[probeər]
to turn (e.g., ~ left)	draai	[drāi]

to underestimate (vt)	onderskat	[ondərskat]
to understand (vt)	verstaan	[ferstān]
to unite (vt)	verenig	[ferenəχ]

to wait (vt)	wag	[vaχ]
to want (wish, desire)	wil	[vil]
to warn (vt)	waarsku	[vãrsku]
to work (vi)	werk	[verk]
to write (vt)	skryf	[skrajf]
to write down	opskryf	[opskrajf]

12. Colors

color	kleur	[kløər]
shade (tint)	skakering	[skakeriŋ]
hue	tint	[tint]
rainbow	reënboog	[reɛn·boəχ]
white (adj)	wit	[vit]
black (adj)	swart	[swart]
gray (adj)	grys	[χrajs]
green (adj)	groen	[χrun]
yellow (adj)	geel	[χeəl]
red (adj)	rooi	[roj]
blue (adj)	blou	[blæʊ]
light blue (adj)	ligblou	[liχ·blæʊ]
pink (adj)	pienk	[pink]
orange (adj)	oranje	[oranje]
violet (adj)	pers	[pers]
brown (adj)	bruin	[brœin]
golden (adj)	goue	[χæʊə]
silvery (adj)	silweragtig	[silweraχtəχ]
beige (adj)	beige	[bɛ:iʒ]
cream (adj)	roomkleurig	[roəm·kløərəχ]
turquoise (adj)	turkoois	[turkojs]
cherry red (adj)	kersierooi	[kersi·roj]
lilac (adj)	lila	[lila]
crimson (adj)	karmosyn	[karmosajn]
light (adj)	lig	[liχ]
dark (adj)	donker	[donkər]
bright, vivid (adj)	helder	[hɛldər]
colored (pencils)	kleurig	[kløərəχ]
color (e.g., ~ film)	kleur	[kløər]
black-and-white (adj)	swart-wit	[swart-wit]
plain (one-colored)	effe	[ɛffə]
multicolored (adj)	veelkleurig	[feəlkløərəχ]

13. Questions

Who?	**Wie?**	[vi?]
What?	**Wat?**	[vat?]
Where? (at, in)	**Waar?**	[vār?]
Where (to)?	**Waarheen?**	[vārheən?]
From where?	**Waarvandaan?**	[vārfandān?]
When?	**Wanneer?**	[vanneər?]
Why? (What for?)	**Hoekom?**	[hukom?]
Why? (~ are you crying?)	**Hoekom?**	[hukom?]
What for?	**Vir wat?**	[fir vat?]
How? (in what way)	**Hoe?**	[hu?]
What? (What kind of ...?)	**Watter?**	[vattər?]
Which?	**Watter een?**	[vattər eən?]
To whom?	**Vir wie?**	[fir vi?]
About whom?	**Oor wie?**	[oər vi?]
About what?	**Oor wat?**	[oər vat?]
With whom?	**Met wie?**	[met vi?]
How many? How much?	**Hoeveel?**	[hufeəl?]

14. Function words. Adverbs. Part 1

Where? (at, in)	**Waar?**	[vār?]
here (adv)	**hier**	[hir]
there (adv)	**daar**	[dār]
somewhere (to be)	**êrens**	[ærɛŋs]
nowhere (not anywhere)	**nêrens**	[nærɛŋs]
by (near, beside)	**by**	[baj]
by the window	**by**	[baj]
Where (to)?	**Waarheen?**	[vārheən?]
here (e.g., come ~!)	**hier**	[hir]
there (e.g., to go ~)	**soontoe**	[soentu]
from here (adv)	**hiervandaan**	[hirfandān]
from there (adv)	**daarvandaan**	[dārfandān]
close (adv)	**naby**	[nabaj]
far (adv)	**ver**	[fer]
near (e.g., ~ Paris)	**naby**	[nabaj]
nearby (adv)	**naby**	[nabaj]
not far (adv)	**nie ver nie**	[ni fər ni]
left (adj)	**linker-**	[linkər-]
on the left	**op linkerhand**	[op linkərhant]

to the left	na links	[na links]
right (adj)	regter	[reҳtər]
on the right	op regterhand	[op reҳtərhant]
to the right	na regs	[na reҳs]
in front (adv)	voor	[foər]
front (as adj)	voorste	[foərstə]
ahead (the kids ran ~)	vooruit	[foərœit]
behind (adv)	agter	[aҳtər]
from behind	van agter	[fan aҳtər]
back (towards the rear)	agtertoe	[aҳtərtu]
middle	middel	[middəl]
in the middle	in die middel	[in di middəl]
at the side	op die sykant	[op di sajkant]
everywhere (adv)	orals	[orals]
around (in all directions)	orals rond	[orals ront]
from inside	van binne	[fan binnə]
somewhere (to go)	êrens	[ærɛŋs]
straight (directly)	reguit	[reҳœit]
back (e.g., come ~)	terug	[teruҳ]
from anywhere	êrens vandaan	[ærɛŋs fandān]
from somewhere	êrens vandaan	[ærɛŋs fandān]
firstly (adv)	in die eerste plek	[in di eərstə plek]
secondly (adv)	in die tweede plek	[in di tweədə plek]
thirdly (adv)	in die derde plek	[in di derdə plek]
suddenly (adv)	skielik	[skilik]
at first (in the beginning)	aan die begin	[ān di beҳin]
for the first time	vir die eerste keer	[fir di eərstə keər]
long before ...	lank voordat ...	[lank foərdat ...]
anew (over again)	opnuut	[opnɪt]
for good (adv)	vir goed	[fir ҳut]
never (adv)	nooit	[nojt]
again (adv)	weer	[veər]
now (adv)	nou	[næʊ]
often (adv)	dikwels	[dikwɛls]
then (adv)	toe	[tu]
urgently (quickly)	dringend	[driŋən]
usually (adv)	gewoonlik	[ҳevoənlik]
by the way, ...	terloops, ...	[terloəps], [...]
possible (that is ~)	moontlik	[moentlik]
probably (adv)	waarskynlik	[vārskajnlik]
maybe (adv)	dalk	[dalk]
besides ...	trouens...	[træʊɛŋs...]

that's why ...	dis hoekom ...	[dis hukom ...]
in spite of ...	ondanks ...	[ondanks ...]
thanks to ...	danksy ...	[danksaj ...]

what (pron.)	wat	[vat]
that (conj.)	dat	[dat]
something	iets	[its]
anything (something)	iets	[its]
nothing	niks	[niks]

who (pron.)	wie	[vi]
someone	iemand	[imant]
somebody	iemand	[imant]

nobody	niemand	[nimant]
nowhere (a voyage to ~)	nêrens	[nærɛŋs]
nobody's	niemand se	[nimant sə]
somebody's	iemand se	[imant sə]

so (I'm ~ glad)	so	[so]
also (as well)	ook	[oək]
too (as well)	ook	[oək]

15. Function words. Adverbs. Part 2

| Why? | Waarom? | [vãrom?] |
| because ... | omdat ... | [omdat ...] |

and	en	[ɛn]
or	of	[of]
but	maar	[mãr]
for (e.g., ~ me)	vir	[fir]

too (~ many people)	te	[te]
only (exclusively)	net	[net]
exactly (adv)	presies	[presis]
about (more or less)	ongeveer	[onχəfeər]

approximately (adv)	ongeveer	[onχəfeər]
approximate (adj)	geraamde	[χerãmdə]
almost (adv)	amper	[ampər]
the rest	die res	[di res]

the other (second)	die ander	[di andər]
other (different)	ander	[andər]
each (adj)	elke	[ɛlkə]
any (no matter which)	enige	[ɛniχə]
many (adv)	baie	[bajə]
much (adv)	baie	[bajə]
many people	baie mense	[bajə mɛŋsə]

all (everyone)	**almal**	[almal]
in return for ...	**in ruil vir...**	[in rœil fir...]
in exchange (adv)	**as vergoeding**	[as ferχudiŋ]
by hand (made)	**met die hand**	[met di hant]
hardly (negative opinion)	**skaars**	[skārs]
probably (adv)	**waarskynlik**	[vārskajnlik]
on purpose (intentionally)	**opsetlik**	[opsetlik]
by accident (adv)	**toevallig**	[tufalleχ]
very (adv)	**baie**	[baje]
for example (adv)	**byvoorbeeld**	[bajfoərbeəlt]
between	**tussen**	[tussən]
among	**tussen**	[tussən]
so much (such a lot)	**so baie**	[so baje]
especially (adv)	**veral**	[feral]

Basic concepts. Part 2

16. Weekdays

Monday	**Maandag**	[mãndaχ]
Tuesday	**Dinsdag**	[dinsdaχ]
Wednesday	**Woensdag**	[voɛŋsdaχ]
Thursday	**Donderdag**	[dondərdaχ]
Friday	**Vrydag**	[frajdaχ]
Saturday	**Saterdag**	[satərdaχ]
Sunday	**Sondag**	[sondaχ]
today (adv)	**vandag**	[fandaχ]
tomorrow (adv)	**môre**	[mɔrə]
the day after tomorrow	**oormôre**	[oərmɔrə]
yesterday (adv)	**gister**	[χistər]
the day before yesterday	**eergister**	[eərχistər]
day	**dag**	[daχ]
working day	**werksdag**	[verks·daχ]
public holiday	**openbare vakansiedag**	[openbarə fakaŋsi·daχ]
day off	**verlofdag**	[ferlofdaχ]
weekend	**naweek**	[naveək]
all day long	**die hele dag**	[di helə daχ]
the next day (adv)	**die volgende dag**	[di folχendə daχ]
two days ago	**twee dae gelede**	[tweə daə χeledə]
the day before	**die dag voor**	[di daχ foər]
daily (adj)	**daeliks**	[daeliks]
every day (adv)	**elke dag**	[ɛlkə daχ]
week	**week**	[veək]
last week (adv)	**laas week**	[lãs veək]
next week (adv)	**volgende week**	[folχendə veək]
weekly (adj)	**weekliks**	[veəkliks]
every week (adv)	**weekliks**	[veəkliks]
every Tuesday	**elke Dinsdag**	[ɛlkə dinsdaχ]

17. Hours. Day and night

morning	**oggend**	[oχent]
in the morning	**soggens**	[soχeŋs]
noon, midday	**middag**	[middaχ]
in the afternoon	**in die namiddag**	[in di namiddaχ]

evening	aand	[ānt]
in the evening	saans	[sāŋs]
night	nag	[naχ]
at night	snags	[snaχs]
midnight	middernag	[middərnaχ]

second	sekonde	[sekondə]
minute	minuut	[minɪt]
hour	uur	[ɪr]
half an hour	n halfuur	[n halfɪr]
fifteen minutes	vyftien minute	[fajftin minutə]
24 hours	24 ure	[fir-en-twintəχ urə]

sunrise	sonop	[son·op]
dawn	daeraad	[daerāt]
early morning	elke oggend	[ɛlkə oχent]
sunset	sononder	[son·ondər]

early in the morning	vroegdag	[fruχdaχ]
this morning	vanmôre	[fanmɔrə]
tomorrow morning	môreoggend	[mɔrə·oχent]

this afternoon	vanmiddag	[fanmiddaχ]
in the afternoon	in die namiddag	[in di namiddaχ]
tomorrow afternoon	môremiddag	[mɔrə·middaχ]

| tonight (this evening) | vanaand | [fanānt] |
| tomorrow night | môreaand | [mɔrə·ānt] |

at 3 o'clock sharp	klokslag 3 uur	[klokslaχ dri ɪr]
about 4 o'clock	omstreeks 4 uur	[omstreeks fir ɪr]
by 12 o'clock	teen 12 uur	[teən twalf ɪr]

| in 20 minutes | oor twintig minute | [oər twintəχ minutə] |
| on time (adv) | betyds | [betajds] |

a quarter of ...	kwart voor ...	[kwart foər ...]
every 15 minutes	elke 15 minute	[ɛlkə fajftin minutə]
round the clock	24 uur per dag	[fir-en-twintəχ pər daχ]

18. Months. Seasons

January	Januarie	[januari]
February	Februarie	[februari]
March	Maart	[mārt]
April	April	[april]
May	Mei	[mæj]
June	Junie	[juni]
July	Julie	[juli]
August	Augustus	[ɔuχustus]

September	**September**	[septembər]
October	**Oktober**	[oktobər]
November	**November**	[nofembər]
December	**Desember**	[desembər]

spring	**lente**	[lentə]
in spring	**in die lente**	[in di lentə]
spring (as adj)	**lente-**	[lente-]

summer	**somer**	[somər]
in summer	**in die somer**	[in di somər]
summer (as adj)	**somerse**	[somersə]

fall	**herfs**	[herfs]
in fall	**in die herfs**	[in di herfs]
fall (as adj)	**herfsagtige**	[herfsaxtixə]

winter	**winter**	[vintər]
in winter	**in die winter**	[in di vintər]
winter (as adj)	**winter-**	[vintər-]

month	**maand**	[mānt]
this month	**hierdie maand**	[hirdi mānt]
next month	**volgende maand**	[folxendə mānt]
last month	**laasmaand**	[lāsmānt]
in 2 months (2 months later)	**oor twe maande**	[oər twə māndə]
the whole month	**die hele maand**	[di helə mānt]

monthly (~ magazine)	**maandeliks**	[māndəliks]
monthly (adv)	**maandeliks**	[māndəliks]
every month	**elke maand**	[ɛlkə mānt]

year	**jaar**	[jār]
this year	**hierdie jaar**	[hirdi jār]
next year	**volgende jaar**	[folxendə jār]
last year	**laasjaar**	[lājār]

| in two years | **binne twee jaar** | [binnə tweə jār] |
| the whole year | **die hele jaar** | [di helə jār] |

every year	**elke jaar**	[ɛlkə jār]
annual (adj)	**jaarliks**	[jārliks]
annually (adv)	**jaarliks**	[jārliks]
4 times a year	**4 keer per jaar**	[fir keər pər jār]

date (e.g., today's ~)	**datum**	[datum]
date (e.g., ~ of birth)	**datum**	[datum]
calendar	**kalender**	[kalendər]
six months	**ses maande**	[ses māndə]
season (summer, etc.)	**seisoen**	[sæjsun]
century	**eeu**	[iʊ]

19. Time. Miscellaneous

time	**tyd**	[tajt]
moment	**moment**	[moment]
instant (n)	**oomblik**	[oəmblik]
instant (adj)	**oombliklik**	[oəmbliklik]
lapse (of time)	**tydbestek**	[tajdbestək]
life	**lewe**	[levə]
eternity	**ewigheid**	[ɛviχæjt]
epoch	**tydperk**	[tajtperk]
era	**tydperk**	[tajtperk]
cycle	**siklus**	[siklus]
period	**periode**	[periodə]
term (short-~)	**termyn**	[termajn]
the future	**die toekoms**	[di tukoms]
future (as adj)	**toekomstig**	[tukomstəχ]
next time	**die volgende keer**	[di folχendə keər]
the past	**die verlede**	[di ferledə]
past (recent)	**laas-**	[lās-]
last time	**die vorige keer**	[di foriχə keər]
later (adv)	**later**	[latər]
after (prep.)	**na**	[na]
nowadays (adv)	**deesdae**	[deəsdaə]
now (adv)	**nou**	[næʊ]
immediately (adv)	**onmiddellik**	[onmiddɛllik]
soon (adv)	**gou**	[χæʊ]
in advance (beforehand)	**by voorbaat**	[baj foərbāt]
a long time ago	**lank gelede**	[lank χeledə]
recently (adv)	**onlangs**	[onlaŋs]
destiny	**noodlot**	[noədlot]
memories (childhood ~)	**herinneringe**	[herinneriŋə]
archives	**argiewe**	[arχivə]
during …	**gedurende …**	[χedurendə …]
long, a long time (adv)	**lank**	[lank]
not long (adv)	**nie lank nie**	[ni lank ni]
early (in the morning)	**vroeg**	[fruχ]
late (not early)	**laat**	[lāt]
forever (for good)	**vir altyd**	[fir altajt]
to start (begin)	**begin**	[beχin]
to postpone (vt)	**uitstel**	[œitstəl]
at the same time	**tegelykertyd**	[teχelajkertajt]
permanently (adv)	**permanent**	[permanent]
constant (noise, pain)	**voortdurend**	[foərtdurent]
temporary (adj)	**tydelik**	[tajdelik]

sometimes (adv)	soms	[soms]
rarely (adv)	selde	[sɛldə]
often (adv)	dikwels	[dikwɛls]

20. Opposites

| rich (adj) | ryk | [rajk] |
| poor (adj) | arm | [arm] |

| ill, sick (adj) | siek | [sik] |
| well (not sick) | gesond | [xesont] |

| big (adj) | groot | [xroət] |
| small (adj) | klein | [klæjn] |

| quickly (adv) | vinnig | [finnəx] |
| slowly (adv) | stadig | [stadəx] |

| fast (adj) | vinnig | [finnəx] |
| slow (adj) | stadig | [stadəx] |

| glad (adj) | bly | [blaj] |
| sad (adj) | droewig | [druvəx] |

| together (adv) | saam | [sãm] |
| separately (adv) | afsonderlik | [afsondərlik] |

| aloud (to read) | hardop | [hardop] |
| silently (to oneself) | stil | [stil] |

| tall (adj) | groot | [xroət] |
| low (adj) | laag | [lãx] |

| deep (adj) | diep | [dip] |
| shallow (adj) | vlak | [flak] |

| yes | ja | [ja] |
| no | nee | [neə] |

| distant (in space) | ver | [fer] |
| nearby (adj) | naby | [nabaj] |

| far (adv) | ver | [fer] |
| nearby (adv) | naby | [nabaj] |

| long (adj) | lang | [laŋ] |
| short (adj) | kort | [kort] |

| good (kindhearted) | vriendelik | [frindəlik] |
| evil (adj) | boos | [boəs] |

| married (adj) | getroud | [χetræʊt] |
| single (adj) | ongetroud | [onχətræʊt] |

| to forbid (vt) | verbied | [ferbit] |
| to permit (vt) | toestaan | [tustãn] |

| end | einde | [æjndə] |
| beginning | begin | [beχin] |

| left (adj) | linker- | [linkər-] |
| right (adj) | regter | [reχtər] |

| first (adj) | eerste | [eerstə] |
| last (adj) | laaste | [lãstə] |

| crime | misdaad | [misdãt] |
| punishment | straf | [straf] |

| to order (vt) | beveel | [befeəl] |
| to obey (vi, vt) | gehoorsaam | [χehoərsãm] |

| straight (adj) | reguit | [reχœit] |
| curved (adj) | krom | [krom] |

| paradise | paradys | [paradajs] |
| hell | hel | [həl] |

| to be born | gebore word | [χeborə vort] |
| to die (vi) | doodgaan | [doədχãn] |

| strong (adj) | sterk | [sterk] |
| weak (adj) | swak | [swak] |

| old (adj) | oud | [æʊt] |
| young (adj) | jong | [joŋ] |

| old (adj) | ou | [æʊ] |
| new (adj) | nuwe | [nuvə] |

| hard (adj) | hard | [hart] |
| soft (adj) | sag | [saχ] |

| warm (tepid) | warm | [varm] |
| cold (adj) | koud | [kæʊt] |

| fat (adj) | vet | [fet] |
| thin (adj) | dun | [dun] |

narrow (adj)	smal	[smal]
wide (adj)	wyd	[vajt]
good (adj)	goed	[χut]
bad (adj)	sleg	[sleχ]

brave (adj)	**dapper**	[dappər]
cowardly (adj)	**lafhartig**	[lafhartəχ]

21. Lines and shapes

square	**vierkant**	[firkant]
square (as adj)	**vierkantig**	[firkantəχ]
circle	**sirkel**	[sirkəl]
round (adj)	**rond**	[ront]
triangle	**driehoek**	[drihuk]
triangular (adj)	**driehoekig**	[drihukəχ]
oval	**ovaal**	[ofãl]
oval (as adj)	**ovaal**	[ofãl]
rectangle	**reghoek**	[reχhuk]
rectangular (adj)	**reghoekig**	[reχhukəχ]
pyramid	**piramide**	[piramidə]
rhombus	**ruit**	[rœit]
trapezoid	**trapesoïed**	[trapesoïət]
cube	**kubus**	[kubus]
prism	**prisma**	[prisma]
circumference	**omtrek**	[omtrək]
sphere	**sfeer**	[sfeər]
ball (solid sphere)	**bal**	[bal]
diameter	**diameter**	[diametər]
radius	**straal**	[strãl]
perimeter (circle's ~)	**omtrek**	[omtrək]
center	**sentrum**	[sentrum]
horizontal (adj)	**horisontaal**	[horisontãl]
vertical (adj)	**vertikaal**	[fertikãl]
parallel (n)	**parallel**	[paralləl]
parallel (as adj)	**parallel**	[paralləl]
line	**lyn**	[lajn]
stroke	**haal**	[hãl]
straight line	**regte lyn**	[reχtə lajn]
curve (curved line)	**krom**	[krom]
thin (line, etc.)	**dun**	[dun]
contour (outline)	**omtrek**	[omtrək]
intersection	**snypunt**	[snaj·punt]
right angle	**regte hoek**	[reχtə huk]
segment	**segment**	[seχment]
sector	**sektor**	[sektor]
side (of triangle)	**sy**	[saj]
angle	**hoek**	[huk]

22. Units of measurement

weight	gewig	[χɛvəχ]
length	lengte	[leŋtə]
width	breedte	[breədtə]
height	hoogte	[hoəχtə]
depth	diepte	[diptə]
volume	volume	[folumə]
area	area	[area]

gram	gram	[χram]
milligram	milligram	[milliχram]
kilogram	kilogram	[kiloχram]
ton	ton	[ton]
pound	pond	[pont]
ounce	ons	[ɔŋs]

meter	meter	[metər]
millimeter	millimeter	[millimetər]
centimeter	sentimeter	[sentimetər]
kilometer	kilometer	[kilometər]
mile	myl	[majl]

inch	duim	[dœim]
foot	voet	[fut]
yard	jaart	[jãrt]

| square meter | vierkante meter | [firkantə metər] |
| hectare | hektaar | [hektãr] |

liter	liter	[litər]
degree	graad	[χrãt]
volt	volt	[folt]

| ampere | ampère | [ampɛ:r] |
| horsepower | perdekrag | [perdə·kraχ] |

| quantity | hoeveelheid | [hufeəlhæjt] |
| half | helfte | [hɛlftə] |

| dozen | dosyn | [dosajn] |
| piece (item) | stuk | [stuk] |

| size | grootte | [χroəttə] |
| scale (map ~) | skaal | [skãl] |

minimal (adj)	minimaal	[minimãl]
the smallest (adj)	die kleinste	[di klæjnstə]
medium (adj)	medium	[medium]
maximal (adj)	maksimaal	[maksimãl]
the largest (adj)	die grootste	[di χroətstə]

23. Containers

canning jar (glass ~)	**glaspot**	[χlas·pot]
can	**blikkie**	[blikki]
bucket	**emmer**	[εmmər]
barrel	**drom**	[drom]
wash basin (e.g., plastic ~)	**wasbak**	[vas·bak]
tank (100L water ~)	**tenk**	[tεnk]
hip flask	**heupfles**	[høəp·fles]
jerrycan	**petrolblik**	[petrol·blik]
tank (e.g., tank car)	**tenk**	[tεnk]
mug	**beker**	[bekər]
cup (of coffee, etc.)	**koppie**	[koppi]
saucer	**piering**	[piriŋ]
glass (tumbler)	**glas**	[χlas]
wine glass	**wynglas**	[vajn·χlas]
stock pot (soup pot)	**soppot**	[sop·pot]
bottle (~ of wine)	**bottel**	[bottəl]
neck (of the bottle, etc.)	**nek**	[nek]
carafe (decanter)	**kraffie**	[kraffi]
pitcher	**kruik**	[krœik]
vessel (container)	**houer**	[hæʊər]
pot (crock, stoneware ~)	**pot**	[pot]
vase	**vaas**	[fãs]
bottle (perfume ~)	**bottel**	[bottəl]
vial, small bottle	**botteltjie**	[bottεlki]
tube (of toothpaste)	**buisie**	[bœisi]
sack (bag)	**sak**	[sak]
bag (paper ~, plastic ~)	**sak**	[sak]
pack (of cigarettes, etc.)	**pakkie**	[pakki]
box (e.g., shoebox)	**kartondoos**	[karton·doəs]
crate	**krat**	[krat]
basket	**mandjie**	[mandʒi]

24. Materials

material	**boustof**	[bæʊstof]
wood (n)	**hout**	[hæʊt]
wood-, wooden (adj)	**hout-**	[hæʊt-]
glass (n)	**glas**	[χlas]
glass (as adj)	**glas-**	[χlas-]

| stone (n) | klip | [klip] |
| stone (as adj) | klip- | [klip-] |

| plastic (n) | plastiek | [plastik] |
| plastic (as adj) | plastiek- | [plastik-] |

| rubber (n) | rubber | [rubbər] |
| rubber (as adj) | rubber- | [rubbər-] |

| cloth, fabric (n) | materiaal | [materiãl] |
| fabric (as adj) | materiaal- | [materiãl-] |

| paper (n) | papier | [papir] |
| paper (as adj) | papier- | [papir-] |

| cardboard (n) | karton | [karton] |
| cardboard (as adj) | karton- | [karton-] |

polyethylene	politeen	[politeən]
cellophane	sellofaan	[sɛllofãn]
linoleum	linoleum	[linoløəm]
plywood	laaghout	[lãχhæʋt]

porcelain (n)	porselein	[porselæjn]
porcelain (as adj)	porselein-	[porselæjn-]
clay (n)	klei	[klæj]
clay (as adj)	klei-	[klæj-]
ceramic (n)	keramiek	[keramik]
ceramic (as adj)	keramiek-	[keramik-]

25. Metals

metal (n)	metaal	[metãl]
metal (as adj)	metaal-	[metãl-]
alloy (n)	allooi	[alloj]

gold (n)	goud	[χæʋt]
gold, golden (adj)	goue	[χæʋə]
silver (n)	silwer	[silwər]
silver (as adj)	silwer-	[silwər-]

iron (n)	yster	[ajstər]
iron-, made of iron (adj)	yster-	[ajstər-]
steel (n)	staal	[stãl]
steel (as adj)	staal-	[stãl-]
copper (n)	koper	[kopər]
copper (as adj)	koper-	[kopər-]

| aluminum (n) | aluminium | [aluminium] |
| aluminum (as adj) | aluminium- | [aluminium-] |

bronze (n)	**brons**	[brɔŋs]
bronze (as adj)	**brons-**	[brɔŋs-]
brass	**geelkoper**	[χeəl·kopər]
nickel	**nikkel**	[nikkəl]
platinum	**platinum**	[platinum]
mercury	**kwik**	[kwik]
tin	**tin**	[tin]
lead	**lood**	[loət]
zinc	**sink**	[sink]

HUMAN BEING

Human being. The body

26. Humans. Basic concepts

human being	mens	[mɛŋs]
man (adult male)	man	[man]
woman	vrou	[fræʊ]
child	kind	[kint]
girl	meisie	[mæjsi]
boy	seun	[søən]
teenager	tiener	[tinər]
old man	ou man	[æʊ man]
old woman	ou vrou	[æʊ fræʊ]

27. Human anatomy

organism (body)	organisme	[orχanismə]
heart	hart	[hart]
blood	bloed	[blut]
artery	slagaar	[slaχãr]
vein	aar	[ãr]
brain	brein	[bræjn]
nerve	senuwee	[senuveə]
nerves	senuwees	[senuveəs]
vertebra	rugwerwels	[ruχ·werwɛls]
spine (backbone)	ruggraat	[ruχ·χrãt]
stomach (organ)	maag	[mãχ]
intestines, bowels	ingewande	[inχəwandə]
intestine (e.g., large ~)	derm	[derm]
liver	lewer	[levər]
kidney	nier	[nir]
bone	been	[beən]
skeleton	geraamte	[χerãmtə]
rib	rib	[rip]
skull	skedel	[skedəl]
muscle	spier	[spir]
biceps	biseps	[biseps]

triceps	**triseps**	[triseps]
tendon	**sening**	[seniŋ]
joint	**gewrig**	[χevrəχ]
lungs	**longe**	[loŋə]
genitals	**geslagsorgane**	[χeslaχs·orχanə]
skin	**vel**	[fəl]

28. Head

head	**kop**	[kop]
face	**gesig**	[χesəχ]
nose	**neus**	[nøøs]
mouth	**mond**	[mont]
eye	**oog**	[oəχ]
eyes	**oë**	[oɛ]
pupil	**pupil**	[pupil]
eyebrow	**wenkbrou**	[vɛnk·bræʊ]
eyelash	**ooghaar**	[oəχ·hăr]
eyelid	**ooglid**	[oəχ·lit]
tongue	**tong**	[toŋ]
tooth	**tand**	[tant]
lips	**lippe**	[lippə]
cheekbones	**wangbene**	[vaŋ·benə]
gum	**tandvleis**	[tand·flæjs]
palate	**verhemelte**	[fer·hemɛltə]
nostrils	**neusgate**	[nøəsχatə]
chin	**ken**	[ken]
jaw	**kakebeen**	[kakebeən]
cheek	**wang**	[vaŋ]
forehead	**voorhoof**	[foərhoəf]
temple	**slaap**	[slăp]
ear	**oor**	[oər]
back of the head	**agterkop**	[aχtərkop]
neck	**nek**	[nek]
throat	**keel**	[keəl]
hair	**haar**	[hăr]
hairstyle	**kapsel**	[kapsəl]
haircut	**haarstyl**	[hărstajl]
wig	**pruik**	[prœik]
mustache	**snor**	[snor]
beard	**baard**	[bărt]
to have (a beard, etc.)	**dra**	[dra]
braid	**vlegsel**	[fleχsəl]
sideburns	**bakkebaarde**	[bakkəbărdə]

red-haired (adj)	**rooiharig**	[roj·harəχ]
gray (hair)	**grys**	[χrajs]
bald (adj)	**kaal**	[kāl]
bald patch	**kaal plek**	[kāl plek]
ponytail	**poniestert**	[poni·stert]
bangs	**gordyntjiekapsel**	[χordajnki·kapsəl]

29. Human body

hand	**hand**	[hant]
arm	**arm**	[arm]
finger	**vinger**	[fiŋər]
toe	**toon**	[toən]
thumb	**duim**	[dœim]
little finger	**pinkie**	[pinki]
nail	**nael**	[naəl]
fist	**vuis**	[fœis]
palm	**palm**	[palm]
wrist	**pols**	[pols]
forearm	**voorarm**	[foərarm]
elbow	**elmboog**	[ɛlmboəχ]
shoulder	**skouer**	[skæʊər]
leg	**been**	[beən]
foot	**voet**	[fut]
knee	**knie**	[kni]
calf (part of leg)	**kuit**	[kœit]
hip	**heup**	[høəp]
heel	**hakskeen**	[hak·skeən]
body	**liggaam**	[liχχām]
stomach	**maag**	[māχ]
chest	**bors**	[bors]
breast	**bors**	[bors]
flank	**sy**	[saj]
back	**rug**	[ruχ]
lower back	**lae rug**	[laə ruχ]
waist	**middel**	[middəl]
navel (belly button)	**naeltjie**	[naɛlki]
buttocks	**boude**	[bæʊdə]
bottom	**sitvlak**	[sitflak]
beauty mark	**moesie**	[musi]
birthmark (café au lait spot)	**moedervlek**	[mudər·flek]
tattoo	**tatoe**	[tatu]
scar	**litteken**	[littekən]

Clothing & Accessories

30. Outerwear. Coats

clothes	klere	[klerə]
outerwear	oorklere	[oərklerə]
winter clothing	winterklere	[vintər·klerə]
coat (overcoat)	jas	[jas]
fur coat	pelsjas	[pelʃas]
fur jacket	kort pelsjas	[kort pelʃas]
down coat	donsjas	[donʃas]
jacket (e.g., leather ~)	baadjie	[bādʒi]
raincoat (trenchcoat, etc.)	reënjas	[reɛnjas]
waterproof (adj)	waterdig	[vatərdeχ]

31. Men's & women's clothing

shirt (button shirt)	hemp	[hemp]
pants	broek	[bruk]
jeans	denimbroek	[denim·bruk]
suit jacket	baadjie	[bādʒi]
suit	pak	[pak]
dress (frock)	rok	[rok]
skirt	romp	[romp]
blouse	bloes	[blus]
knitted jacket (cardigan, etc.)	gebreide baadjie	[χebræjdə bādʒi]
jacket (of woman's suit)	baadjie	[bādʒi]
T-shirt	T-hemp	[te-hemp]
shorts (short trousers)	kortbroek	[kort·bruk]
tracksuit	sweetpak	[sweet·pak]
bathrobe	badjas	[batjas]
pajamas	pajama	[pajama]
sweater	trui	[trœi]
pullover	trui	[trœi]
vest	onderbaadjie	[ondər·bādʒi]
tailcoat	swaelstertbaadjie	[swaɛlstert·bādʒi]
tuxedo	aandpak	[āntpak]

uniform	**uniform**	[uniform]
workwear	**werksklere**	[verks·klerə]
overalls	**oorpak**	[oərpak]
coat (e.g., doctor's smock)	**jas**	[jas]

32. Clothing. Underwear

underwear	**onderklere**	[ondərklerə]
boxers, briefs	**onderbroek**	[ondərbruk]
panties	**onderbroek**	[ondərbruk]
undershirt (A-shirt)	**frokkie**	[frokki]
socks	**sokkies**	[sokkis]

nightgown	**nagrok**	[naχrok]
bra	**bra**	[bra]
knee highs	**kniekouse**	[kni·kæʊsə]
(knee-high socks)		

pantyhose	**kousbroek**	[kæʊsbruk]
stockings (thigh highs)	**kouse**	[kæʊsə]
bathing suit	**baaikostuum**	[bãj·kostɪm]

33. Headwear

hat	**hoed**	[hut]
fedora	**hoed**	[hut]
baseball cap	**bofbalpet**	[bofbal·pet]
flatcap	**pet**	[pet]

beret	**mus**	[mus]
hood	**kap**	[kap]
panama hat	**panamahoed**	[panama·hut]
knit cap (knitted hat)	**gebreide mus**	[χebræjdə mus]

headscarf	**kopdoek**	[kopduk]
women's hat	**dameshoed**	[dames·hut]
hard hat	**veiligheidshelm**	[fæjliχæjts·hɛlm]
garrison cap	**mus**	[mus]
helmet	**helmet**	[hɛlmet]

| derby | **bolhoed** | [bolhut] |
| top hat | **hoëhoed** | [hoɛhut] |

34. Footwear

| footwear | **skoeisel** | [skuisəl] |
| shoes (men's shoes) | **mansskoene** | [maŋs·skunə] |

shoes (women's shoes)	damesskoene	[dames·skunə]
boots (e.g., cowboy ~)	laarse	[lārsə]
slippers	pantoffels	[pantoffəls]

tennis shoes (e.g., Nike ~)	tennisskoene	[tɛnnis·skunə]
sneakers	tekkies	[tɛkkis]
(e.g., Converse ~)		
sandals	sandale	[sandalə]

cobbler (shoe repairer)	skoenmaker	[skun·makər]
heel	hak	[hak]
pair (of shoes)	paar	[pār]

shoestring	skoenveter	[skun·fetər]
to lace (vt)	ryg	[rajχ]
shoehorn	skoenlepel	[skun·lepəl]
shoe polish	skoenpolitoer	[skun·politur]

35. Textile. Fabrics

cotton (n)	katoen	[katun]
cotton (as adj)	katoen-	[katun-]
flax (n)	vlas	[flas]
flax (as adj)	vlas-	[flas-]

silk (n)	sy	[saj]
silk (as adj)	sy-	[saj-]
wool (n)	wol	[vol]
wool (as adj)	wol-	[vol-]

velvet	fluweel	[fluveəl]
suede	suède	[suɛdə]
corduroy	ferweel	[ferweəl]

nylon (n)	nylon	[najlon]
nylon (as adj)	nylon-	[najlon-]
polyester (n)	poliëster	[poliɛstər]
polyester (as adj)	poliëster-	[poliɛstər-]

leather (n)	leer	[leər]
leather (as adj)	leer-	[leər-]
fur (n)	bont	[bont]
fur (e.g., ~ coat)	bont-	[bont-]

36. Personal accessories

| gloves | handskoene | [handskunə] |
| mittens | duimhandskoene | [dœim·handskunə] |

scarf (muffler)	**serp**	[serp]
glasses (eyeglasses)	**bril**	[bril]
frame (eyeglass ~)	**raam**	[rãm]
umbrella	**sambreel**	[sambreəl]
walking stick	**wandelstok**	[vandəl·stok]
hairbrush	**haarborsel**	[hãr·borsəl]
fan	**waaier**	[vãjer]

tie (necktie)	**das**	[das]
bow tie	**strikkie**	[strikki]
suspenders	**kruisbande**	[krœis·bandə]
handkerchief	**sakdoek**	[sakduk]

comb	**kam**	[kam]
barrette	**haarspeld**	[hãrs·pɛlt]
hairpin	**haarpen**	[hãr·pen]
buckle	**gespe**	[χespə]

belt	**belt**	[bɛlt]
shoulder strap	**skouerband**	[skæʋer·bant]

bag (handbag)	**handsak**	[hand·sak]
purse	**beursie**	[bøərsi]
backpack	**rugsak**	[ruχsak]

37. Clothing. Miscellaneous

fashion	**mode**	[modə]
in vogue (adj)	**in die mode**	[in di modə]
fashion designer	**modeontwerper**	[modə·ontwerpər]

collar	**kraag**	[krãχ]
pocket	**sak**	[sak]
pocket (as adj)	**sak-**	[sak-]
sleeve	**mou**	[mæʋ]
hanging loop	**lussie**	[lussi]
fly (on trousers)	**gulp**	[χulp]

zipper (fastener)	**ritssluiter**	[rits·slœiter]
fastener	**vasmaker**	[fasmakər]
button	**knoop**	[knoəp]
buttonhole	**knoopsgat**	[knoəps·χat]
to come off (ab. button)	**loskom**	[loskom]

to sew (vi, vt)	**naai**	[nãi]
to embroider (vi, vt)	**borduur**	[bordɪr]
embroidery	**borduurwerk**	[bordɪr·werk]
sewing needle	**naald**	[nãlt]
thread	**garing**	[χariŋ]
seam	**soom**	[soəm]

to get dirty (vi)	vuil word	[fœil vort]
stain (mark, spot)	vlek	[flek]
to crease, crumple (vi)	kreukel	[krøəkəl]
to tear, to rip (vt)	skeur	[skøər]
clothes moth	mot	[mot]

38. Personal care. Cosmetics

toothpaste	tandepasta	[tandə·pasta]
toothbrush	tandeborsel	[tandə·borsəl]
to brush one's teeth	tande borsel	[tandə borsəl]
razor	skeermes	[skeər·mes]
shaving cream	skeerroom	[skeər·roəm]
to shave (vi)	skeer	[skeər]
soap	seep	[seəp]
shampoo	sjampoe	[ʃampu]
scissors	skêr	[skær]
nail file	naelvyl	[naɛl·fajl]
nail clippers	naelknipper	[naɛl·knippər]
tweezers	haartangetjie	[hãrtaŋəki]
cosmetics	kosmetika	[kosmetika]
face mask	gesigmasker	[χesiχ·maskər]
manicure	manikuur	[manikɪr]
to have a manicure	laat manikuur	[lãt manikɪr]
pedicure	voetbehandeling	[fut·behandeliŋ]
make-up bag	kosmetika tassie	[kosmetika tassi]
face powder	gesigpoeier	[χesiχ·pujer]
powder compact	poeierdosie	[pujer·dosi]
blusher	blosser	[blossər]
perfume (bottled)	parfuum	[parfɪm]
toilet water (lotion)	reukwater	[røək·vatər]
lotion	vloeiroom	[flui·roəm]
cologne	reukwater	[røək·vatər]
eyeshadow	oogskadu	[oəχ·skadu]
eyeliner	oogomlyner	[oəχ·omlajnər]
mascara	maskara	[maskara]
lipstick	lipstiffie	[lip·stiffi]
nail polish, enamel	naellak	[naɛl·lak]
hair spray	haarsproei	[hãrs·prui]
deodorant	reukweermiddel	[røək·veərmiddəl]
cream	room	[roəm]
face cream	gesigroom	[χesiχ·roəm]

hand cream	handroom	[hand·roəm]
anti-wrinkle cream	antirimpelroom	[antirimpəl·roəm]
day cream	dagroom	[daχ·roəm]
night cream	nagroom	[naχ·roəm]
day (as adj)	dag-	[daχ-]
night (as adj)	nag-	[naχ-]

tampon	tampon	[tampon]
toilet paper (toilet roll)	toiletpapier	[tojlet·papir]
hair dryer	haardroër	[hār·droɛr]

39. Jewelry

jewelry	juweliersware	[juvelirs·warə]
precious (e.g., ~ stone)	edel-	[ɛdəl-]
hallmark stamp	waarmerk	[vārmerk]

ring	ring	[riŋ]
wedding ring	trouring	[træʊriŋ]
bracelet	armband	[armbant]

earrings	oorbelle	[oər·bɛllə]
necklace (~ of pearls)	halssnoer	[hals·snur]
crown	kroon	[kroən]
bead necklace	kraalsnoer	[krāl·snur]

diamond	diamant	[diamant]
emerald	smarag	[smaraχ]
ruby	robyn	[robajn]
sapphire	saffier	[saffir]
pearl	pêrel	[pæerəl]
amber	amber	[ambər]

40. Watches. Clocks

watch (wristwatch)	polshorlosie	[pols·horlosi]
dial	wyserplaat	[vajsər·plāt]
hand (of clock, watch)	wyster	[vajstər]
metal watch band	metaal horlosiebandjie	[metāl horlosi·bandʒi]
watch strap	horlosiebandjie	[horlosi·bandʒi]

battery	battery	[battəraj]
to be dead (battery)	pap wees	[pap veəs]
to run fast	voorloop	[foərloəp]
to run slow	agterloop	[aχtərloəp]

wall clock	muurhorlosie	[mɪr·horlosi]
hourglass	uurglas	[ɪr·χlas]

sundial	**sonwyser**	[son·wajsər]
alarm clock	**wekker**	[vɛkkər]
watchmaker	**horlosiemaker**	[horlosi·makər]
to repair (vt)	**herstel**	[herstəl]

Food. Nutricion

41. Food

meat	vleis	[flæjs]
chicken	hoender	[hundər]
Rock Cornish hen (poussin)	braaikuiken	[brāj·kœiken]
duck	eend	[eent]
goose	gans	[χaŋs]
game	wild	[vilt]
turkey	kalkoen	[kalkun]
pork	varkvleis	[fark·flæjs]
veal	kalfsvleis	[kalfs·flæjs]
lamb	lamsvleis	[lams·flæjs]
beef	beesvleis	[bees·flæjs]
rabbit	konynvleis	[konajn·flæjs]
sausage (bologna, pepperoni, etc.)	wors	[vors]
vienna sausage (frankfurter)	Weense worsie	[veɛŋsə vorsi]
bacon	spek	[spek]
ham	ham	[ham]
gammon	gerookte ham	[χeroəktə ham]
pâté	patee	[pateə]
liver	lewer	[levər]
hamburger (ground beef)	maalvleis	[māl·flæjs]
tongue	tong	[toŋ]
egg	eier	[æjer]
eggs	eiers	[æjers]
egg white	eierwit	[æjer·wit]
egg yolk	dooier	[dojer]
fish	vis	[fis]
seafood	seekos	[seə·kos]
crustaceans	skaaldiere	[skāldirə]
caviar	kaviaar	[kafiār]
crab	krab	[krap]
shrimp	garnaal	[χarnāl]
oyster	oester	[ustər]
spiny lobster	seekreef	[seə·kreəf]

octopus	**seekat**	[seə·kat]
squid	**pylinkvis**	[pajl·inkfis]
sturgeon	**steur**	[støər]
salmon	**salm**	[salm]
halibut	**heilbot**	[hæjlbot]
cod	**kabeljou**	[kabeljæʊ]
mackerel	**makriel**	[makril]
tuna	**tuna**	[tuna]
eel	**paling**	[paliŋ]
trout	**forel**	[forəl]
sardine	**sardyn**	[sardajn]
pike	**varswatersnoek**	[farswatər·snuk]
herring	**haring**	[hariŋ]
bread	**brood**	[broət]
cheese	**kaas**	[kãs]
sugar	**suiker**	[sœikər]
salt	**sout**	[sæʊt]
rice	**rys**	[rajs]
pasta (macaroni)	**pasta**	[pasta]
noodles	**noedels**	[nudɛls]
butter	**botter**	[bottər]
vegetable oil	**plantaardige olie**	[plantãrdiχə oli]
sunflower oil	**sonblomolie**	[sonblom·oli]
margarine	**margarien**	[marχarin]
olives	**olywe**	[olajvə]
olive oil	**olyfolie**	[olajf·oli]
milk	**melk**	[mɛlk]
condensed milk	**kondensmelk**	[kondɛŋs·mɛlk]
yogurt	**jogurt**	[joχurt]
sour cream	**suurroom**	[sɪr·roəm]
cream (of milk)	**room**	[roəm]
mayonnaise	**mayonnaise**	[majonɛs]
buttercream	**crème**	[krɛm]
cereal grains (wheat, etc.)	**ontbytgraan**	[ontbajt·χrãn]
flour	**meelblom**	[meəl·blom]
canned food	**blikkieskos**	[blikkis·kos]
cornflakes	**mielievlokkies**	[mili·flokkis]
honey	**heuning**	[høəniŋ]
jam	**konfyt**	[konfajt]
chewing gum	**kougom**	[kæʊχom]

42. Drinks

water	**water**	[vatər]
drinking water	**drinkwater**	[drink·vatər]
mineral water	**mineraalwater**	[minerāl·vatər]
still (adj)	**sonder gas**	[sonder χas]
carbonated (adj)	**soda-**	[soda-]
sparkling (adj)	**bruis-**	[brœis-]
ice	**ys**	[ajs]
with ice	**met ys**	[met ajs]
non-alcoholic (adj)	**nie-alkoholies**	[ni-alkoholis]
soft drink	**koeldrank**	[kul·drank]
refreshing drink	**verfrissende drank**	[ferfrissendə drank]
lemonade	**limonade**	[limonadə]
liquors	**likeure**	[likøərə]
wine	**wyn**	[vajn]
white wine	**witwyn**	[vit·vajn]
red wine	**rooiwyn**	[roj·vajn]
liqueur	**likeur**	[likøər]
champagne	**sjampanje**	[ʃampanje]
vermouth	**vermoet**	[fermut]
whiskey	**whisky**	[vhiskaj]
vodka	**vodka**	[fodka]
gin	**jenever**	[jenefər]
cognac	**brandewyn**	[brandə·vajn]
rum	**rum**	[rum]
coffee	**koffie**	[koffi]
black coffee	**swart koffie**	[swart koffi]
coffee with milk	**koffie met melk**	[koffi met melk]
cappuccino	**capuccino**	[kaputʃino]
instant coffee	**poeierkoffie**	[pujer·koffi]
milk	**melk**	[melk]
cocktail	**mengeldrankie**	[menχəl·dranki]
milkshake	**melkskommel**	[melk·skomməl]
juice	**sap**	[sap]
tomato juice	**tamatiesap**	[tamati·sap]
orange juice	**lemoensap**	[lemoən·sap]
freshly squeezed juice	**vars geparste sap**	[fars χeparstə sap]
beer	**bier**	[bir]
light beer	**ligte bier**	[liχtə bir]
dark beer	**donker bier**	[donker bir]
tea	**tee**	[teə]

| black tea | **swart tee** | [swart teə] |
| green tea | **groen tee** | [χrun teə] |

43. Vegetables

| vegetables | **groente** | [χruntə] |
| greens | **groente** | [χruntə] |

tomato	**tamatie**	[tamati]
cucumber	**komkommer**	[komkommər]
carrot	**wortel**	[vortəl]
potato	**aartappel**	[ãrtappəl]
onion	**ui**	[œi]
garlic	**knoffel**	[knoffəl]

cabbage	**kool**	[koəl]
cauliflower	**blomkool**	[blom·koəl]
Brussels sprouts	**Brusselspruite**	[brussɛl·sprœeitə]
broccoli	**broccoli**	[brokoli]

beetroot	**beet**	[beət]
eggplant	**eiervrug**	[æejerfruχ]
zucchini	**vingerskorsie**	[fiŋər·skorsi]
pumpkin	**pampoen**	[pampun]
turnip	**raap**	[rãp]

parsley	**pietersielie**	[pitərsili]
dill	**dille**	[dillə]
lettuce	**slaai**	[slãi]
celery	**seldery**	[selderaj]
asparagus	**aspersie**	[aspersi]
spinach	**spinasie**	[spinasi]

pea	**ertjie**	[ɛrki]
beans	**boontjies**	[boənkis]
corn (maize)	**mielie**	[mili]
kidney bean	**nierboontjie**	[nir·boənki]

bell pepper	**paprika**	[paprika]
radish	**radys**	[radajs]
artichoke	**artisjok**	[artiʃok]

44. Fruits. Nuts

fruit	**vrugte**	[fruχtə]
apple	**appel**	[appəl]
pear	**peer**	[peər]
lemon	**suurlemoen**	[sɪr·lemun]

| orange | lemoen | [lemun] |
| strawberry (garden ~) | aarbei | [ārbæj] |

mandarin	nartjie	[narki]
plum	pruim	[prœim]
peach	perske	[perskə]
apricot	appelkoos	[appɛlkoəs]
raspberry	framboos	[framboəs]
pineapple	pynappel	[pajnappəl]

banana	piesang	[pisaŋ]
watermelon	waatlemoen	[vātlemun]
grape	druif	[drœif]
cherry	kersie	[kersi]
sour cherry	suurkersie	[sɪr·kersi]
sweet cherry	soetkersie	[sut·kersi]
melon	spanspek	[spaŋspek]

grapefruit	pomelo	[pomelo]
avocado	avokado	[afokado]
papaya	papaja	[papaja]
mango	mango	[manχo]
pomegranate	granaat	[χranāt]

redcurrant	rooi aalbessie	[roj ālbɛssi]
blackcurrant	swartbessie	[swartbɛssi]
gooseberry	appelliefie	[appɛllifi]
bilberry	bosbessie	[bosbɛssi]
blackberry	braambessie	[brāmbɛssi]

raisin	rosyntjie	[rosajnki]
fig	vy	[faj]
date	dadel	[dadəl]

peanut	grondboontjie	[χront·boənki]
almond	amandel	[amandəl]
walnut	okkerneut	[okkər·nøət]
hazelnut	haselneut	[hasɛl·nøət]
coconut	klapper	[klappər]
pistachios	pistachio	[pistatʃio]

45. Bread. Candy

bakers' confectionery (pastry)	soet gebak	[sut χebak]
bread	brood	[broət]
cookies	koekies	[kukis]

| chocolate (n) | sjokolade | [ʃokoladə] |
| chocolate (as adj) | sjokolade | [ʃokoladə] |

candy (wrapped)	**lekkers**	[lɛkkərs]
cake (e.g., cupcake)	**koek**	[kuk]
cake (e.g., birthday ~)	**koek**	[kuk]

pie (e.g., apple ~)	**pastei**	[pastæj]
filling (for cake, pie)	**vulsel**	[fulsəl]

jam (whole fruit jam)	**konfyt**	[konfajt]
marmalade	**marmelade**	[marmeladə]
waffles	**wafels**	[vafɛls]
ice-cream	**roomys**	[roəm·ajs]
pudding	**poeding**	[pudiŋ]

46. Cooked dishes

course, dish	**gereg**	[χerəχ]
cuisine	**kookkuns**	[koək·kuns]
recipe	**resep**	[resep]
portion	**porsie**	[porsi]

salad	**slaai**	[slãi]
soup	**sop**	[sop]

clear soup (broth)	**helder sop**	[hɛldər sop]
sandwich (bread)	**toebroodjie**	[tubroədʒi]
fried eggs	**gabakte eiers**	[χabaktə æjers]

hamburger (beefburger)	**hamburger**	[hamburχər]
beefsteak	**biefstuk**	[bifstuk]

side dish	**sygereg**	[saj·χerəχ]
spaghetti	**spaghetti**	[spaχɛtti]
mashed potatoes	**kapokaartappels**	[kapok·ãrtappəls]
pizza	**pizza**	[pizza]
porridge (oatmeal, etc.)	**pap**	[pap]
omelet	**omelet**	[oməlet]

boiled (e.g., ~ beef)	**gekook**	[χekoək]
smoked (adj)	**gerook**	[χeroək]
fried (adj)	**gebak**	[χebak]
dried (adj)	**gedroog**	[χedroəχ]
frozen (adj)	**gevries**	[χefris]
pickled (adj)	**gepiekel**	[χepikəl]

sweet (sugary)	**soet**	[sut]
salty (adj)	**sout**	[sæʊt]
cold (adj)	**koud**	[kæʊt]
hot (adj)	**warm**	[varm]
bitter (adj)	**bitter**	[bittər]
tasty (adj)	**smaaklik**	[smãklik]

to cook in boiling water	kook in water	[koək in vatər]
to cook (dinner)	kook	[koək]
to fry (vt)	braai	[braj]
to heat up (food)	opwarm	[opwarm]

to salt (vt)	sout	[sæʊt]
to pepper (vt)	peper	[pepər]
to grate (vt)	rasp	[rasp]
peel (n)	skil	[skil]
to peel (vt)	skil	[skil]

47. Spices

salt	sout	[sæʊt]
salty (adj)	sout	[sæʊt]
to salt (vt)	sout	[sæʊt]

black pepper	swart peper	[swart pepər]
red pepper (milled ~)	rooi peper	[roj pepər]
mustard	mosterd	[mostert]
horseradish	peperwortel	[peper·wortəl]

condiment	smaakmiddel	[smāk·middəl]
spice	spesery	[spesəraj]
sauce	sous	[sæʊs]
vinegar	asyn	[asajn]

anise	anys	[anajs]
basil	basilikum	[basilikum]
cloves	naeltjies	[naɛlkis]
ginger	gemmer	[χemmər]
coriander	koljander	[koljandər]
cinnamon	kaneel	[kaneəl]

sesame	sesamsaad	[sesam·sāt]
bay leaf	lourierblaar	[læʊrir·blār]
paprika	paprika	[paprika]
caraway	komynsaad	[komajnsāt]
saffron	saffraan	[saffrān]

48. Meals

food	kos	[kos]
to eat (vi, vt)	eet	[eet]

breakfast	ontbyt	[ontbajt]
to have breakfast	ontbyt	[ontbajt]
lunch	middagete	[middaχ·etə]

to have lunch	gaan eet	[χān eət]
dinner	aandete	[āndetə]
to have dinner	aandete gebruik	[āndetə χebrœik]

| appetite | aptyt | [aptajt] |
| Enjoy your meal! | Smaaklike ete! | [smāklikə etə!] |

to open (~ a bottle)	oopmaak	[oəpmāk]
to spill (liquid)	mors	[mors]
to spill out (vi)	mors	[mors]

to boil (vi)	kook	[koək]
to boil (vt)	kook	[koək]
boiled (~ water)	gekook	[χekoək]

| to chill, cool down (vt) | laat afkoel | [lāt afkul] |
| to chill (vi) | afkoel | [afkul] |

| taste, flavor | smaak | [smāk] |
| aftertaste | nasmaak | [nasmāk] |

to slim down (lose weight)	vermaer	[fermaər]
diet	dieet	[diət]
vitamin	vitamien	[fitamin]
calorie	kalorie	[kalori]

| vegetarian (n) | vegetariër | [feχetariɛr] |
| vegetarian (adj) | vegetaries | [feχetaris] |

fats (nutrient)	vette	[fɛttə]
proteins	proteïen	[proteïen]
carbohydrates	koolhidrate	[koəlhidratə]

slice (of lemon, ham)	snytjie	[snajki]
piece (of cake, pie)	stuk	[stuk]
crumb (of bread, cake, etc.)	krummel	[krumməl]

49. Table setting

spoon	lepel	[lepəl]
knife	mes	[mes]
fork	vurk	[furk]

| cup (e.g., coffee ~) | koppie | [koppi] |
| plate (dinner ~) | bord | [bort] |

saucer	piering	[piriŋ]
napkin (on table)	servet	[serfət]
toothpick	tandestokkie	[tandə·stokki]

50. Restaurant

restaurant	**restaurant**	[restɔurant]
coffee house	**koffiekroeg**	[koffi·kruχ]
pub, bar	**kroeg**	[kruχ]
tearoom	**teekamer**	[teə·kamər]
waiter	**kelner**	[kɛlnər]
waitress	**kelnerin**	[kɛlnərin]
bartender	**kroegman**	[kruχman]
menu	**spyskaart**	[spajs·kãrt]
wine list	**wyn**	[vajn]
to book a table	**wynkaart**	[vajn·kãrt]
course, dish	**gereg**	[χerəχ]
to order (meal)	**bestel**	[bestəl]
to make an order	**bestel**	[bestəl]
aperitif	**drankie**	[dranki]
appetizer	**voorgereg**	[foərχerəχ]
dessert	**nagereg**	[naχerəχ]
check	**rekening**	[rekəniŋ]
to pay the check	**die rekening betaal**	[di rekəniŋ betãl]
to give change	**kleingeld gee**	[klæjn·χɛlt χeə]
tip	**fooitjie**	[fojki]

Family, relatives and friends

51. Personal information. Forms

name (first name)	**voornaam**	[foərnãm]
surname (last name)	**van**	[fan]
date of birth	**geboortedatum**	[χeboərtə·datum]
place of birth	**geboorteplek**	[χeboərtə·plek]
nationality	**nasionaliteit**	[naʃionalitæjt]
place of residence	**woonplek**	[voən·plek]
country	**land**	[lant]
profession (occupation)	**beroep**	[berup]
gender, sex	**geslag**	[χeslaχ]
height	**lengte**	[leŋtə]
weight	**gewig**	[χeveχ]

52. Family members. Relatives

mother	**moeder**	[mudər]
father	**vader**	[fadər]
son	**seun**	[søən]
daughter	**dogter**	[doχtər]
younger daughter	**jonger dogter**	[joŋər doχtər]
younger son	**jonger seun**	[joŋər søən]
eldest daughter	**oudste dogter**	[æʊdstə doχtər]
eldest son	**oudste seun**	[æʊdstə søən]
brother	**broer**	[brur]
elder brother	**ouer broer**	[æʊer brur]
younger brother	**jonger broer**	[joŋər brur]
sister	**suster**	[sustər]
elder sister	**ouer suster**	[æʊer sustər]
younger sister	**jonger suster**	[joŋər sustər]
cousin (masc.)	**neef**	[neəf]
cousin (fem.)	**neef**	[neəf]
mom, mommy	**ma**	[ma]
dad, daddy	**pa**	[pa]
parents	**ouers**	[æʊers]
child	**kind**	[kint]
children	**kinders**	[kindərs]

grandmother	**ouma**	[æʊma]
grandfather	**oupa**	[æʊpa]
grandson	**kleinseun**	[klæjn·søøn]
granddaughter	**kleindogter**	[klæjn·doχtər]
grandchildren	**kleinkinders**	[klæjn·kindərs]
uncle	**oom**	[oəm]
aunt	**tante**	[tantə]
nephew	**neef**	[neəf]
niece	**nig**	[niχ]
mother-in-law (wife's mother)	**skoonma**	[skoən·ma]
father-in-law (husband's father)	**skoonpa**	[skoən·pa]
son-in-law (daughter's husband)	**skoonseun**	[skoən·søøn]
stepmother	**stiefma**	[stifma]
stepfather	**stiefpa**	[stifpa]
infant	**baba**	[baba]
baby (infant)	**baba**	[baba]
little boy, kid	**seuntjie**	[søønki]
wife	**vrou**	[fræʊ]
husband	**man**	[man]
spouse (husband)	**eggenoot**	[ɛχχenoət]
spouse (wife)	**eggenote**	[ɛχχenotə]
married (masc.)	**getroud**	[χetræʊt]
married (fem.)	**getroud**	[χetræʊt]
single (unmarried)	**ongetroud**	[onχətræʊt]
bachelor	**vrygesel**	[frajχesəl]
divorced (masc.)	**geskei**	[χeskæj]
widow	**weduwee**	[veduveə]
widower	**wedunaar**	[vedunār]
relative	**familielid**	[famililit]
close relative	**na familie**	[na famili]
distant relative	**ver familie**	[fer famili]
relatives	**familielede**	[famililedə]
orphan (boy or girl)	**weeskind**	[veəskint]
guardian (of a minor)	**voog**	[foəχ]
to adopt (a boy)	**aanneem**	[ānneəm]
to adopt (a girl)	**aanneem**	[ānneəm]

53. Friends. Coworkers

friend (masc.)	**vriend**	[frint]
friend (fem.)	**vriendin**	[frindin]

| friendship | vriendskap | [frindskap] |
| to be friends | bevriend wees | [befrint veəs] |

buddy (masc.)	maat	[mãt]
buddy (fem.)	vriendin	[frindin]
partner	maat	[mãt]

chief (boss)	baas	[bãs]
superior (n)	baas	[bãs]
owner, proprietor	eienaar	[æjenãr]
subordinate (n)	ondergeskikte	[ondərχeskiktə]
colleague	kollega	[kolleχa]

acquaintance (person)	kennis	[kɛnnis]
fellow traveler	medereisiger	[medə·ræjsiχər]
classmate	klasmaat	[klas·mãt]

neighbor (masc.)	buurman	[bɪrman]
neighbor (fem.)	buurvrou	[bɪrfræʋ]
neighbors	bure	[burə]

54. Man. Woman

woman	vrou	[fræʋ]
girl (young woman)	meisie	[mæjsi]
bride	bruid	[brœit]

beautiful (adj)	mooi	[moj]
tall (adj)	groot	[χroət]
slender (adj)	slank	[slank]
short (adj)	kort	[kort]

| blonde (n) | blondine | [blondinə] |
| brunette (n) | brunet | [brunet] |

ladies' (adj)	dames-	[dames-]
virgin (girl)	maagd	[mãχt]
pregnant (adj)	swanger	[swaŋər]

man (adult male)	man	[man]
blond (n)	blond	[blont]
brunet (n)	brunet	[brunet]
tall (adj)	groot	[χroət]
short (adj)	kort	[kort]

rude (rough)	onbeskof	[onbeskof]
stocky (adj)	frisgebou	[frisχebæʋ]
robust (adj)	frisgebou	[frisχebæʋ]
strong (adj)	sterk	[sterk]
strength	sterkte	[sterktə]

stout, fat (adj)	vet	[fet]
swarthy (adj)	blas	[blas]
slender (well-built)	slank	[slank]
elegant (adj)	elegant	[ɛleχant]

55. Age

age	ouderdom	[æʋderdom]
youth (young age)	jeug	[jøeχ]
young (adj)	jong	[joŋ]

| younger (adj) | jonger | [joŋər] |
| older (adj) | ouer | [æʋer] |

young man	jongman	[joŋman]
teenager	tiener	[tinər]
guy, fellow	ou	[æʋ]

| old man | ou man | [æʋ man] |
| old woman | ou vrou | [æʋ fræʋ] |

adult (adj)	volwasse	[folwassə]
middle-aged (adj)	middeljarig	[middəl·jarəχ]
elderly (adj)	bejaard	[bejārt]
old (adj)	oud	[æʋt]

retirement	pensioen	[pɛnsiun]
to retire (from job)	met pensioen gaan	[met pɛnsiun χān]
retiree	pensioenaris	[pɛnsiunaris]

56. Children

child	kind	[kint]
children	kinders	[kindərs]
twins	tweeling	[tweeliŋ]

cradle	wiegie	[viχi]
rattle	rammelaar	[rammelār]
diaper	luier	[lœiər]

pacifier	fopspeen	[fopspeən]
baby carriage	kinderwaentjie	[kindər·waenki]
kindergarten	kindertuin	[kindər·tœin]
babysitter	babasitter	[babasittər]

childhood	kinderdae	[kindərdaə]
doll	pop	[pop]
toy	speelgoed	[speəl·χut]

construction set (toy)	boudoos	[bæʊ·doəs]
well-bred (adj)	goed opgevoed	[χut opχəfut]
ill-bred (adj)	sleg opgevoed	[sleχ opχəfut]
spoiled (adj)	bederf	[bederf]

to be naughty	stout wees	[stæʊt veəs]
mischievous (adj)	ondeuend	[ondøent]
mischievousness	ondeuendheid	[ondøenthæjt]
mischievous child	rakker	[rakkər]

| obedient (adj) | gehoorsaam | [χehoərsām] |
| disobedient (adj) | ongehoorsaam | [onχəhoərsām] |

docile (adj)	soet	[sut]
clever (smart)	slim	[slim]
child prodigy	wonderkind	[vondərkint]

57. Married couples. Family life

to kiss (vt)	soen	[sun]
to kiss (vi)	mekaar soen	[mekār sun]
family (n)	familie	[famili]
family (as adj)	gesins-	[χesins-]
couple	paartjie	[pārki]
marriage (state)	huwelik	[huvelik]
hearth (home)	tuiste	[tœistə]
dynasty	dinastie	[dinasti]

| date | datum | [datum] |
| kiss | soen | [sun] |

love (for sb)	liefde	[lifdə]
to love (sb)	liefhë	[lifhɛ:]
beloved	geliefde	[χelifdə]

tenderness	teerheid	[teərhæjt]
tender (affectionate)	teer	[teər]
faithfulness	trou	[træʊ]
faithful (adj)	trou	[træʊ]
care (attention)	sorg	[sorχ]
caring (~ father)	sorgsaam	[sorχsām]

newlyweds	pasgetroudes	[pas·χetræʊdes]
honeymoon	wittebroodsdae	[vittebroəds·daə]
to get married (ab. woman)	trou	[træʊ]
to get married (ab. man)	trou	[træʊ]

| wedding | bruilof | [brœilof] |
| golden wedding | goue bruilof | [χæʊə brœilof] |

anniversary	**verjaardag**	[ferjār·daχ]
lover (masc.)	**minnaar**	[minnãr]
mistress (lover)	**minnares**	[minnares]
adultery	**owerspel**	[overspəl]
to cheat on ... (commit adultery)	**owerspel pleeg**	[overspəl pleeχ]
jealous (adj)	**jaloers**	[jalurs]
to be jealous	**jaloers wees**	[jalurs veəs]
divorce	**egskeiding**	[εχskæjdiŋ]
to divorce (vi)	**skei**	[skæj]
to quarrel (vi)	**baklei**	[baklæj]
to be reconciled (after an argument)	**versoen**	[fersun]
together (adv)	**saam**	[sām]
sex	**seks**	[seks]
happiness	**geluk**	[χeluk]
happy (adj)	**gelukkig**	[χelukkəχ]
misfortune (accident)	**ongeluk**	[onχəluk]
unhappy (adj)	**ongelukkig**	[onχəlukkəχ]

Character. Feelings. Emotions

58. Feelings. Emotions

feeling (emotion)	gevoel	[χeful]
feelings	gevoelens	[χefulɛŋs]
to feel (vt)	voel	[ful]
hunger	honger	[hoŋər]
to be hungry	honger wees	[hoŋər veəs]
thirst	dors	[dors]
to be thirsty	dors wees	[dors veəs]
sleepiness	slaperigheid	[slaperiχæjt]
to feel sleepy	vaak voel	[fãk ful]
tiredness	moegheid	[muχæjt]
tired (adj)	moeg	[muχ]
to get tired	moeg word	[muχ vort]
mood (humor)	stemming	[stɛmmiŋ]
boredom	verveling	[ferfeliŋ]
to be bored	verveeld wees	[ferveəlt veəs]
seclusion	afsondering	[afsondəriŋ]
to seclude oneself	jou afsonder	[jæʊ afsondər]
to worry (make anxious)	bekommerd maak	[bekommərt mãk]
to be worried	bekommerd wees	[bekommərt veəs]
worrying (n)	kommerwekkend	[kommər·wɛkkent]
anxiety	vrees	[freəs]
preoccupied (adj)	behep	[behep]
to be nervous	senuweeagtig wees	[senuveə·aχtəχ veəs]
to panic (vi)	paniekerig raak	[panikerəχ rãk]
hope	hoop	[hoəp]
to hope (vi, vt)	hoop	[hoəp]
certainty	sekerheid	[sekərhæjt]
certain, sure (adj)	seker	[sekər]
uncertainty	onsekerheid	[ɔŋsekərhæjt]
uncertain (adj)	onseker	[ɔŋsekər]
drunk (adj)	dronk	[dronk]
sober (adj)	nugter	[nuχtər]
weak (adj)	swak	[swak]
happy (adj)	gelukkig	[χelukkəχ]
to scare (vt)	bang maak	[baŋ mãk]

| fury (madness) | kwaadheid | [kwãdhæjt] |
| rage (fury) | woede | [vudə] |

depression	depressie	[deprɛssi]
discomfort (unease)	ongemak	[onχəmak]
comfort	gemak	[χemak]
to regret (be sorry)	jammer wees	[jammər veəs]
regret	spyt	[spajt]
bad luck	teëspoed	[teɛsput]
sadness	droefheid	[drufhæjt]

shame (remorse)	skaamte	[skãmtə]
gladness	vreugde	[frøəχdə]
enthusiasm, zeal	entoesiasme	[ɛntusiasmə]
enthusiast	entoesiasties	[ɛntusiastis]
to show enthusiasm	begeestering toon	[beχeəsteriŋ toən]

59. Character. Personality

character	karakter	[karaktər]
character flaw	karakterfout	[karaktər·fæʊt]
mind	verstand	[ferstant]
reason	verstand	[ferstant]

conscience	gewete	[χevetə]
habit (custom)	gewoonte	[χevoentə]
ability (talent)	talent	[talent]
can (e.g., ~ swim)	kan	[kan]

patient (adj)	geduldig	[χeduldəχ]
impatient (adj)	ongeduldig	[onχəduldəχ]
curious (inquisitive)	nuuskierig	[nɪskirəχ]
curiosity	nuuskierigheid	[nɪskiriχæjt]

modesty	beskeidenheid	[beskæjdenhæjt]
modest (adj)	beskeie	[beskæje]
immodest (adj)	onbeskeie	[onbeskæje]

laziness	luiheid	[lœihæjt]
lazy (adj)	lui	[lœi]
lazy person (masc.)	luiaard	[lœiãrt]

cunning (n)	sluheid	[sluhæjt]
cunning (as adj)	slu	[slu]
distrust	wantroue	[vantræʊə]
distrustful (adj)	agterdogtig	[aχtərdoχtəχ]

generosity	gulheid	[χulhæjt]
generous (adj)	gulhartig	[χulhartəχ]
talented (adj)	talentvol	[talentfol]

talent	**talent**	[talent]
courageous (adj)	**moedig**	[mudəχ]
courage	**moed**	[mut]
honest (adj)	**eerlik**	[eərlik]
honesty	**eerlikheid**	[eərlikhæjt]

careful (cautious)	**versigtig**	[fersiχtəχ]
brave (courageous)	**dapper**	[dappər]
serious (adj)	**ernstig**	[ɛrnstəχ]
strict (severe, stern)	**streng**	[streŋ]

decisive (adj)	**vasberade**	[fasberadə]
indecisive (adj)	**besluiteloos**	[beslœiteloəs]
shy, timid (adj)	**skaam**	[skãm]
shyness, timidity	**skaamheid**	[skãmhæjt]

confidence (trust)	**vertroue**	[fertræʊə]
to believe (trust)	**vertrou**	[fertræʊ]
trusting (credulous)	**goedgelowig**	[χudχəlovəχ]

sincerely (adv)	**opreg**	[opreχ]
sincere (adj)	**opregte**	[opreχtə]
sincerity	**opregtheid**	[opreχthæjt]
open (person)	**oop**	[oəp]

calm (adj)	**kalm**	[kalm]
frank (sincere)	**openhartig**	[openhartəχ]
naïve (adj)	**naïef**	[naïef]
absent-minded (adj)	**verstrooid**	[ferstrojt]
funny (odd)	**snaaks**	[snãks]

greed	**hebsug**	[hebsuχ]
greedy (adj)	**hebsugtig**	[hebsuχtəχ]
stingy (adj)	**gierig**	[χirəχ]
evil (adj)	**boos**	[boəs]
stubborn (adj)	**hardnekkig**	[hardnɛkkəχ]
unpleasant (adj)	**onaangenaam**	[onãnχənãm]

selfish person (masc.)	**selfsugtig**	[sɛlfsuχtəχ]
selfish (adj)	**selfsugtig**	[sɛlfsuχtəχ]
coward	**laffaard**	[laffãrt]
cowardly (adj)	**lafhartig**	[lafhartəχ]

60. Sleep. Dreams

to sleep (vi)	**slaap**	[slãp]
sleep, sleeping	**slaap**	[slãp]
dream	**droom**	[droəm]
to dream (in sleep)	**droom**	[droəm]
sleepy (adj)	**vaak**	[fãk]

bed	**bed**	[bet]
mattress	**matras**	[matras]
blanket (comforter)	**kombers**	[kombers]
pillow	**kussing**	[kussiŋ]
sheet	**laken**	[laken]

insomnia	**slaaploosheid**	[slāploəshæjt]
sleepless (adj)	**slaaploos**	[slāploəs]
sleeping pill	**slaappil**	[slāp·pil]

to feel sleepy	**vaak voel**	[fāk ful]
to yawn (vi)	**gaap**	[χāp]
to go to bed	**gaan slaap**	[χān slāp]
to make up the bed	**die bed opmaak**	[di bet opmāk]
to fall asleep	**aan die slaap raak**	[ān di slāp rāk]

nightmare	**nagmerrie**	[naχmerri]
snore, snoring	**gesnork**	[χesnork]
to snore (vi)	**snork**	[snork]

alarm clock	**wekker**	[vɛkkər]
to wake (vt)	**wakker maak**	[vakkər māk]
to wake up	**wakker word**	[vakkər vort]
to get up (vi)	**opstaan**	[opstān]
to wash up (wash face)	**jou was**	[jæʊ vas]

61. Humour. Laughter. Gladness

humor (wit, fun)	**humor**	[humor]
sense of humor	**humorsin**	[humorsin]
to enjoy oneself	**jouself geniet**	[jæʊsɛlf χenit]
cheerful (merry)	**vrolik**	[frolik]
merriment (gaiety)	**pret**	[pret]

| smile | **glimlag** | [χlimlaχ] |
| to smile (vi) | **glimlag** | [χlimlaχ] |

to start laughing	**begin lag**	[beχin laχ]
to laugh (vi)	**lag**	[laχ]
laugh, laughter	**lag**	[laχ]

anecdote	**anekdote**	[anekdotə]
funny (anecdote, etc.)	**snaaks**	[snāks]
funny (odd)	**snaaks**	[snāks]

to joke (vi)	**grappies maak**	[χrappis māk]
joke (verbal)	**grappie**	[χrappi]
joy (emotion)	**vreugde**	[frøəχdə]
to rejoice (vi)	**bly wees**	[blaj veəs]
joyful (adj)	**bly**	[blaj]

62. Discussion, conversation. Part 1

communication	**kommunikasie**	[kommunikasi]
to communicate	**kommunikeer**	[kommunikeər]
conversation	**gesprek**	[χesprek]
dialog	**dialoog**	[dialoəχ]
discussion (discourse)	**diskussie**	[diskussi]
dispute (debate)	**dispuut**	[dispɪt]
to dispute	**debatteer**	[debatteər]
interlocutor	**gespreksgenoot**	[χespreks·χenoət]
topic (theme)	**onderwerp**	[ondərwerp]
point of view	**standpunt**	[stand·punt]
opinion (point of view)	**opinie**	[opini]
speech (talk)	**toespraak**	[tusprãk]
discussion (of report, etc.)	**bespreking**	[besprekiŋ]
to discuss (vt)	**bespreek**	[bespreək]
talk (conversation)	**gesprek**	[χesprek]
to talk (to chat)	**gesels**	[χesɛls]
meeting	**ontmoeting**	[ontmutiŋ]
to meet (vi, vt)	**ontmoet**	[ontmut]
proverb	**spreekwoord**	[spreək·woərt]
saying	**gesegde**	[χeseχdə]
riddle (poser)	**raaisel**	[rãjsəl]
password	**wagwoord**	[vaχ·woərt]
secret	**geheim**	[χəhæjm]
oath (vow)	**eed**	[eət]
to swear (an oath)	**sweer**	[sweər]
promise	**belofte**	[beloftə]
to promise (vt)	**beloof**	[beloəf]
advice (counsel)	**raad**	[rãt]
to advise (vt)	**aanraai**	[ãnrãi]
to follow one's advice	**raad volg**	[rãt folχ]
to listen to ... (obey)	**luister na**	[lœistər na]
news	**nuus**	[nɪs]
sensation (news)	**sensasie**	[sɛŋsasi]
information (data)	**inligting**	[inliχtiŋ]
conclusion (decision)	**slotsom**	[slotsom]
voice	**stem**	[stem]
compliment	**kompliment**	[kompliment]
kind (nice)	**gaaf**	[χãf]
word	**woord**	[voərt]
phrase	**frase**	[frasə]
answer	**antwoord**	[antwoərt]

| truth | **waarheid** | [vārhæjt] |
| lie | **leuen** | [løəen] |

thought	**gedagte**	[χedaχtə]
idea (inspiration)	**idee**	[ideə]
fantasy	**verbeelding**	[ferbeəldiŋ]

63. Discussion, conversation. Part 2

respected (adj)	**gerespekteer**	[χerespekteər]
to respect (vt)	**respekteer**	[respekteər]
respect	**respek**	[respek]
Dear ... (letter)	**Geagte ...**	[χeaχtə ...]

| to introduce (sb to sb) | **voorstel** | [foərstəl] |
| to make acquaintance | **kennismaak** | [kɛnnismāk] |

intention	**voorneme**	[foərnemə]
to intend (have in mind)	**voornemens wees**	[foərnemɛŋs veəs]
wish	**wens**	[vɛŋs]
to wish (~ good luck)	**wens**	[vɛŋs]

surprise (astonishment)	**verrassing**	[ferrassiŋ]
to surprise (amaze)	**verras**	[ferras]
to be surprised	**verbaas wees**	[ferbās veəs]

to give (vt)	**gee**	[χeə]
to take (get hold of)	**vat**	[fat]
to give back	**teruggee**	[teruχeə]
to return (give back)	**terugvat**	[teruχfat]

to apologize (vi)	**verskoning vra**	[ferskoniŋ fra]
apology	**verskoning**	[ferskoniŋ]
to forgive (vt)	**vergewe**	[ferχevə]

to talk (speak)	**praat**	[prāt]
to listen (vi)	**luister**	[lœistər]
to hear out	**aanhoor**	[ānhoər]
to understand (vt)	**verstaan**	[ferstān]

to show (to display)	**wys**	[vajs]
to look at ...	**kyk na ...**	[kajk na ...]
to call (yell for sb)	**roep**	[rup]
to distract (disturb)	**aflei**	[aflæj]
to disturb (vt)	**steur**	[støər]
to pass (to hand sth)	**deurgee**	[døərχeə]

demand (request)	**versoek**	[fersuk]
to request (ask)	**versoek**	[fersuk]
demand (firm request)	**eis**	[æjs]

to demand (request firmly)	eis	[æjs]
to tease (call names)	terg	[terχ]
to mock (make fun of)	terg	[terχ]
mockery, derision	spot	[spot]
nickname	bynaam	[bajnãm]

insinuation	sinspeling	[sinspeliŋ]
to insinuate (imply)	sinspeel	[sinspeəl]
to mean (vt)	impliseer	[impliseər]

description	beskrywing	[beskrajviŋ]
to describe (vt)	beskryf	[beskrajf]
praise (compliments)	lof	[lof]
to praise (vt)	loof	[loəf]

disappointment	teleurstelling	[teløərstɛliŋ]
to disappoint (vt)	teleurstel	[teløərstəl]
to be disappointed	teleurgestel	[teløərχestəl]

supposition	veronderstelling	[feronderstɛliŋ]
to suppose (assume)	veronderstel	[feronderstəl]
warning (caution)	waarskuwing	[vãrskuviŋ]
to warn (vt)	waarsku	[vãrsku]

64. Discussion, conversation. Part 3

| to talk into (convince) | ompraat | [omprãt] |
| to calm down (vt) | kalmeer | [kalmeər] |

silence (~ is golden)	stilte	[stiltə]
to be silent (not speaking)	stilbly	[stilblaj]
to whisper (vi, vt)	fluister	[flœistər]
whisper	gefluister	[χeflœistər]

| frankly, sincerely (adv) | openlik | [openlik] |
| in my opinion ... | volgens my ... | [folχɛŋs maj ...] |

detail (of the story)	besonderhede	[besondərhedə]
detailed (adj)	gedetailleerd	[χedetajlleərt]
in detail (adv)	in detail	[in detajl]
hint, clue	wenk	[vɛnk]

look (glance)	kykie	[kajki]
to have a look	kyk	[kajk]
fixed (look)	strak	[strak]
to blink (vi)	knipper	[knippər]
to wink (vi)	knipoog	[knipoəχ]
to nod (in assent)	knik	[knik]
sigh	sug	[suχ]
to sigh (vi)	sug	[suχ]

to shudder (vi)	huiwer	[hœivər]
gesture	gebaar	[χebãr]
to touch (one's arm, etc.)	aanraak	[ãnrãk]
to seize (e.g., ~ by the arm)	vat	[fat]
to tap (on the shoulder)	op die skouer tik	[op di skæʊər tik]

Look out!	Oppas!	[oppas!]
Really?	Regtig?	[reχtəχ?]
Are you sure?	Is jy seker?	[is jaj sekər?]
Good luck!	Voorspoed!	[foərspud!]
I see!	Ek sien!	[ɛk sin!]
What a pity!	Jammer!	[jammər!]

65. Agreement. Refusal

consent	toelating	[tulatiŋ]
to consent (vi)	toelaat	[tulãt]
approval	goedkeuring	[χudkøəriŋ]
to approve (vt)	goedkeur	[χudkøər]

refusal	weiering	[væjeriŋ]
to refuse (vi, vt)	weier	[væjer]

Great!	Wonderlik!	[vondərlik!]
All right!	Goed!	[χud!]
Okay! (I agree)	OK!	[okej!]

forbidden (adj)	verbode	[ferbodə]
it's forbidden	dit is verbode	[dit is ferbodə]
it's impossible	dis onmoontlik	[dis onmoentlik]
incorrect (adj)	onjuis	[onjœis]

to reject (~ a demand)	verwerp	[ferwerp]
to support (cause, idea)	steun	[støən]
to accept (~ an apology)	aanvaar	[ãnfãr]

to confirm (vt)	bevestig	[befestəχ]
confirmation	bevestiging	[befestəχiŋ]
permission	toelating	[tulatiŋ]
to permit (vt)	toelaat	[tulãt]

decision	besluit	[beslœit]
to say nothing (hold one's tongue)	stilbly	[stilblaj]

condition (term)	voorwaarde	[foərwãrdə]
excuse (pretext)	verskoning	[ferskoniŋ]
praise (compliments)	lof	[lof]
to praise (vt)	loof	[loəf]

66. Success. Good luck. Failure

success	sukses	[suksɛs]
successfully (adv)	suksesvol	[suksɛsfol]
successful (adj)	suksesvol	[suksɛsfol]
luck (good luck)	geluk	[χeluk]
Good luck!	Voorspoed!	[foərspud!]
lucky (e.g., ~ day)	geluks-	[χeluks-]
lucky (fortunate)	gelukkig	[χelukkəχ]
failure	mislukking	[mislukkiŋ]
misfortune	teëspoed	[teɛsput]
bad luck	teëspoed	[teɛsput]
unsuccessful (adj)	onsuksesvol	[ɔŋsuksɛsfol]
catastrophe	katastrofe	[katastrofə]
pride	trots	[trots]
proud (adj)	trots	[trots]
to be proud	trots wees	[trots veəs]
winner	wenner	[vɛnnər]
to win (vi)	wen	[ven]
to lose (not win)	verloor	[ferloər]
try	probeerslag	[probeərslaχ]
to try (vi)	probeer	[probeər]
chance (opportunity)	kans	[kaŋs]

67. Quarrels. Negative emotions

shout (scream)	skreeu	[skriʊ]
to shout (vi)	skreeu	[skriʊ]
to start to cry out	begin skreeu	[beχin skriʊ]
quarrel	rusie	[rusi]
to quarrel (vi)	baklei	[baklæj]
fight (squabble)	stryery	[strajeraj]
to make a scene	spektakel maak	[spektakəl māk]
conflict	konflik	[konflik]
misunderstanding	misverstand	[misferstant]
insult	belediging	[beledəχiŋ]
to insult (vt)	beledig	[beledəχ]
insulted (adj)	beledig	[beledəχ]
resentment	gekrenktheid	[χekrɛnkthæjt]
to offend (vt)	beledig	[beledəχ]
to take offense	gekrenk voel	[χekrɛnk ful]
indignation	verontwaardiging	[ferontwārdəχiŋ]
to be indignant	verontwaardig wees	[ferontwārdəχ veəs]

complaint	klag	[klaχ]
to complain (vi, vt)	kla	[kla]

apology	verskoning	[ferskoniŋ]
to apologize (vi)	verskoning vra	[ferskoniŋ fra]
to beg pardon	om verskoning vra	[om ferskoniŋ fra]

criticism	kritiek	[kritik]
to criticize (vt)	kritiseer	[kritiseər]
accusation	beskuldiging	[beskuldəχiŋ]
to accuse (vt)	beskuldig	[beskuldəχ]

revenge	wraak	[vrãk]
to avenge (get revenge)	wreek	[vreək]
to pay back	wraak neem	[vrãk neəm]

disdain	minagting	[minaχtiŋ]
to despise (vt)	minag	[minaχ]
hatred, hate	haat	[hãt]
to hate (vt)	haat	[hãt]

nervous (adj)	senuweeagtig	[senuveə·aχtəχ]
to be nervous	senuweeagtig wees	[senuveə·aχtəχ veəs]
angry (mad)	kwaad	[kwãt]
to make angry	kwaad maak	[kwãt mãk]

humiliation	vernedering	[fernedəriŋ]
to humiliate (vt)	verneder	[fernedər]
to humiliate oneself	jouself verneder	[jæusɛlf fernedər]

shock	skok	[skok]
to shock (vt)	skok	[skok]

trouble (e.g., serious ~)	probleme	[probləmə]
unpleasant (adj)	onaangenaam	[onãnχənãm]

fear (dread)	vrees	[freəs]
terrible (storm, heat)	verskriklik	[ferskriklik]
scary (e.g., ~ story)	vreesaanjaend	[freəsãnjaent]
horror	afgryse	[afχrajsə]
awful (crime, news)	vreeslik	[freəslik]

to begin to tremble	begin beef	[beχin beəf]
to cry (weep)	huil	[hœil]
to start crying	begin huil	[beχin hœil]
tear	traan	[trãn]

fault	skuld	[skult]
guilt (feeling)	skuldgevoel	[skultχəful]
dishonor (disgrace)	skande	[skandə]
protest	protes	[protes]
stress	stres	[stres]

to disturb (vt)	**steur**	[støər]
to be furious	**woedend wees**	[vudent veəs]
mad, angry (adj)	**kwaad**	[kwãt]
to end (~ a relationship)	**beëindig**	[beɛindəx]
to swear (at sb)	**sweer**	[sweər]
to scare (become afraid)	**skrik**	[skrik]
to hit (strike with hand)	**slaan**	[slãn]
to fight (street fight, etc.)	**baklei**	[baklæj]
to settle (a conflict)	**besleg**	[besleχ]
discontented (adj)	**ontevrede**	[ontefredə]
furious (adj)	**woedend**	[vudent]
It's not good!	**Dis nie goed nie!**	[dis ni χut ni!]
It's bad!	**Dis sleg!**	[dis sleχ!]

Medicine

68. Diseases

sickness	siekte	[siktə]
to be sick	siek wees	[sik veəs]
health	gesondheid	[χesonthæjt]

runny nose (coryza)	loopneus	[loəpnøəs]
tonsillitis	keelontsteking	[keəl·ontstekiŋ]
cold (illness)	verkoue	[ferkæʊə]

bronchitis	bronchitis	[bronχitis]
pneumonia	longontsteking	[loŋ·ontstekiŋ]
flu, influenza	griep	[χrip]

nearsighted (adj)	bysiende	[bajsində]
farsighted (adj)	versiende	[fersində]
strabismus (crossed eyes)	skeelheid	[skeəlhæjt]
cross-eyed (adj)	skeel	[skeəl]
cataract	katarak	[katarak]
glaucoma	gloukoom	[χlæʊkoəm]

stroke	beroerte	[berurtə]
heart attack	hartaanval	[hart·ānfal]
myocardial infarction	hartinfark	[hart·infark]
paralysis	verlamming	[ferlammiŋ]
to paralyze (vt)	verlam	[ferlam]

allergy	allergie	[allerχi]
asthma	asma	[asma]
diabetes	suikersiekte	[sœikər·siktə]

| toothache | tandpyn | [tand·pajn] |
| caries | tandbederf | [tand·bederf] |

diarrhea	diarree	[diarreə]
constipation	hardlywigheid	[hardlajviχæjt]
stomach upset	maagongesteldheid	[māχ·oŋəstɛldhæjt]
food poisoning	voedselvergiftiging	[fudsəl·ferχiftəχiŋ]
to get food poisoning	voedselvergiftiging kry	[fudsəl·ferχiftəχiŋ kraj]

arthritis	artritis	[artritis]
rickets	Engelse siekte	[ɛŋəlsə siktə]
rheumatism	reumatiek	[røəmatik]
atherosclerosis	artrosklerose	[artrosklerosə]

77

gastritis	**maagontsteking**	[mãχ·ontstekiŋ]
appendicitis	**blindedermontsteking**	[blindəderm·ontstekiŋ]
cholecystitis	**galblaasontsteking**	[χalblãs·ontstekiŋ]
ulcer	**maagsweer**	[mãχsweər]
measles	**masels**	[masɛls]
rubella (German measles)	**Duitse masels**	[dœitsə masɛls]
jaundice	**geelsug**	[χeəlsuχ]
hepatitis	**hepatitis**	[hepatitis]
schizophrenia	**skisofrenie**	[skisofreni]
rabies (hydrophobia)	**hondsdolheid**	[hondsdolhæjt]
neurosis	**neurose**	[nøərosə]
concussion	**harsingskudding**	[harsiŋ·skuddiŋ]
cancer	**kanker**	[kankər]
sclerosis	**sklerose**	[sklerosə]
multiple sclerosis	**veelvuldige sklerose**	[feəlfuldiχə sklerosə]
alcoholism	**alkoholisme**	[alkoholismə]
alcoholic (n)	**alkoholikus**	[alkoholikus]
syphilis	**sifilis**	[sifilis]
AIDS	**VIGS**	[vigs]
tumor	**tumor**	[tumor]
malignant (adj)	**kwaadaardig**	[kwãdãrdəχ]
benign (adj)	**goedaardig**	[χudãrdəχ]
fever	**koors**	[koərs]
malaria	**malaria**	[malaria]
gangrene	**gangreen**	[χanχreən]
seasickness	**seesiekte**	[seə·siktə]
epilepsy	**epilepsie**	[ɛpilepsi]
epidemic	**epidemie**	[ɛpidemi]
typhus	**tifus**	[tifus]
tuberculosis	**tuberkulose**	[tuberkulosə]
cholera	**cholera**	[χolera]
plague (bubonic ~)	**pes**	[pes]

69. Symptoms. Treatments. Part 1

symptom	**simptoom**	[simptoəm]
temperature	**temperatuur**	[temperatɪr]
high temperature (fever)	**koors**	[koərs]
pulse	**polsslag**	[pols·slaχ]
dizziness (vertigo)	**duiseligheid**	[dœiseliχæjt]
hot (adj)	**warm**	[varm]
shivering	**koue rillings**	[kæʊə rilliŋs]

pale (e.g., ~ face)	bleek	[bleək]
cough	hoes	[hus]
to cough (vi)	hoes	[hus]
to sneeze (vi)	nies	[nis]
faint	floute	[flæʊtə]
to faint (vi)	flou word	[flæʊ vort]
bruise (hématome)	blou kol	[blæʊ kol]
bump (lump)	knop	[knop]
to bang (bump)	stamp	[stamp]
contusion (bruise)	besering	[beseriŋ]
to limp (vi)	hink	[hink]
dislocation	ontwrigting	[ontwriχtiŋ]
to dislocate (vt)	ontwrig	[ontwrəχ]
fracture	breuk	[brøək]
to have a fracture	n breuk hê	[n brøək hɛ:]
cut (e.g., paper ~)	sny	[snaj]
to cut oneself	jouself sny	[jæʊsɛlf snaj]
bleeding	bloeding	[bludiŋ]
burn (injury)	brandwond	[brant·vont]
to get burned	jouself brand	[jæʊsɛlf brant]
to prick (vt)	prik	[prik]
to prick oneself	jouself prik	[jæʊsɛlf prik]
to injure (vt)	seermaak	[seərmāk]
injury	besering	[beseriŋ]
wound	wond	[vont]
trauma	trauma	[trɔuma]
to be delirious	yl	[ajl]
to stutter (vi)	stotter	[stottər]
sunstroke	sonsteek	[sɔŋ·steək]

70. Symptoms. Treatments. Part 2

pain, ache	pyn	[pajn]
splinter (in foot, etc.)	splinter	[splintər]
sweat (perspiration)	sweet	[sweət]
to sweat (perspire)	sweet	[sweət]
vomiting	braak	[brāk]
convulsions	stuiptrekkings	[stœip·trɛkkiŋs]
pregnant (adj)	swanger	[swaŋər]
to be born	gebore word	[χeborə vort]
delivery, labor	geboorte	[χeboərtə]
to deliver (~ a baby)	baar	[bār]

abortion	**aborsie**	[aborsi]
breathing, respiration	**asemhaling**	[asemhaliŋ]
in-breath (inhalation)	**inaseming**	[inasemiŋ]
out-breath (exhalation)	**uitaseming**	[œitasemiŋ]
to exhale (breathe out)	**uitasem**	[œitasem]
to inhale (vi)	**inasem**	[inasem]

disabled person	**invalide**	[infalidə]
cripple	**kreupel**	[krøəpəl]
drug addict	**dwelmslaaf**	[dwɛlm·slāf]

deaf (adj)	**doof**	[doəf]
mute (adj)	**stom**	[stom]
deaf mute (adj)	**doofstom**	[doəf·stom]

mad, insane (adj)	**swaksinnig**	[swaksinnəχ]
madman (demented person)	**kranksinnige**	[kranksinniχə]
madwoman	**kranksinnige**	[kranksinniχə]
to go insane	**kranksinnig word**	[kranksinnəχ vort]

gene	**geen**	[χeən]
immunity	**immuniteit**	[immunitæjt]
hereditary (adj)	**erflik**	[ɛrflik]
congenital (adj)	**aangebore**	[ānχəborə]

virus	**virus**	[firus]
microbe	**mikrobe**	[mikrobə]
bacterium	**bakterie**	[bakteri]
infection	**infeksie**	[infeksi]

71. Symptoms. Treatments. Part 3

| hospital | **hospitaal** | [hospitāl] |
| patient | **pasiënt** | [pasiɛnt] |

diagnosis	**diagnose**	[diaχnosə]
cure	**genesing**	[χenesiŋ]
medical treatment	**mediese behandeling**	[medisə behandəliŋ]
to get treatment	**behandeling kry**	[behandəliŋ kraj]
to treat (~ a patient)	**behandel**	[behandəl]
to nurse (look after)	**versorg**	[fersorχ]
care (nursing ~)	**versorging**	[fersorχiŋ]

operation, surgery	**operasie**	[operasi]
to bandage (head, limb)	**verbind**	[ferbint]
bandaging	**verband**	[ferbant]

| vaccination | **inenting** | [inɛntiŋ] |
| to vaccinate (vt) | **inent** | [inɛnt] |

injection, shot	inspuiting	[inspœitiŋ]
attack	aanval	[ãnfal]
amputation	amputasie	[amputasi]
to amputate (vt)	amputeer	[amputeer]
coma	koma	[koma]
intensive care	intensiewe sorg	[intɛnsivə sorχ]

to recover (~ from flu)	herstel	[herstəl]
condition (patient's ~)	kondisie	[kondisi]
consciousness	bewussyn	[bevussajn]
memory (faculty)	geheue	[χəhøə]

to pull out (tooth)	trek	[trek]
filling	vulsel	[fulsəl]
to fill (a tooth)	vul	[ful]

| hypnosis | hipnose | [hipnosə] |
| to hypnotize (vt) | hipnotiseer | [hipnotiseer] |

72. Doctors

doctor	dokter	[doktər]
nurse	verpleegster	[ferpleeχ·stər]
personal doctor	lyfarts	[lajf·arts]

dentist	tandarts	[tand·arts]
eye doctor	oogarts	[oeχ·arts]
internist	internis	[internis]
surgeon	chirurg	[ʃirurχ]

psychiatrist	psigiater	[psiχiatər]
pediatrician	kinderdokter	[kindər·doktər]
psychologist	sielkundige	[silkundiχə]
gynecologist	ginekoloog	[χinekoloəχ]
cardiologist	kardioloog	[kardioloəχ]

73. Medicine. Drugs. Accessories

medicine, drug	medisyn	[medisajn]
remedy	geneesmiddel	[χeneəs·middəl]
to prescribe (vt)	voorskryf	[foərskrajf]
prescription	voorskrif	[foərskrif]

tablet, pill	pil	[pil]
ointment	salf	[salf]
ampule	ampul	[ampul]
mixture	mengsel	[meŋsəl]
syrup	stroop	[stroəp]

| pill | pil | [pil] |
| powder | poeier | [pujer] |

gauze bandage	verband	[ferbant]
cotton wool	watte	[vattə]
iodine	iodium	[iodium]

Band-Aid	pleister	[plæjstər]
eyedropper	oogdrupper	[oəχ·druppər]
thermometer	termometer	[termometər]
syringe	spuitnaald	[spœit·nält]

| wheelchair | rolstoel | [rol·stul] |
| crutches | krukke | [krukkə] |

painkiller	pynstiller	[pajn·stillər]
laxative	lakseermiddel	[lakseər·middəl]
spirits (ethanol)	spiritus	[spiritus]
medicinal herbs	geneeskragtige kruie	[χeneəs·kraχtiχə krœiə]
herbal (~ tea)	kruie-	[krœie-]

74. Smoking. Tobacco products

tobacco	tabak	[tabak]
cigarette	sigaret	[siχaret]
cigar	sigaar	[siχār]
pipe	pyp	[pajp]
pack (of cigarettes)	pakkie	[pakki]

matches	vuurhoutjies	[fɪrhæʊkis]
matchbox	vuurhoutjiedosie	[fɪrhæʊki·dosi]
lighter	aansteker	[ãŋstekər]
ashtray	asbak	[asbak]
cigarette case	sigarethouer	[siχaret·hæʊər]

| cigarette holder | sigaretpypie | [siχaret·pajpi] |
| filter (cigarette tip) | filter | [filtər] |

to smoke (vi, vt)	rook	[roək]
to light a cigarette	aansteek	[ãŋsteək]
smoking	rook	[roək]
smoker	roker	[rokər]

stub, butt (of cigarette)	stompie	[stompi]
smoke, fumes	rook	[roək]
ash	as	[as]

HUMAN HABITAT

City

75. City. Life in the city

city, town	stad	[stat]
capital city	hoofstad	[hoəf·stat]
village	dorp	[dorp]

city map	stadskaart	[stats·kārt]
downtown	sentrum	[sentrum]
suburb	voorstad	[foərstat]
suburban (adj)	voorstedelik	[foərstedelik]

outskirts	buitewyke	[bœitevajke]
environs (suburbs)	omgewing	[omχeviŋ]
city block	stadswyk	[stats·wajk]
residential block (area)	woonbuurt	[voənbɪrt]

traffic	verkeer	[ferkeər]
traffic lights	robot	[robot]
public transportation	openbare vervoer	[openbare ferfur]
intersection	kruispunt	[krœis·punt]

crosswalk	sebraoorgang	[sebra·oərχaŋ]
pedestrian underpass	voetgangertonnel	[futχaŋər·tonnəl]
to cross (~ the street)	oorsteek	[oərsteək]
pedestrian	voetganger	[futχaŋər]
sidewalk	sypaadjie	[saj·pādʒi]

bridge	brug	[bruχ]
embankment (river walk)	wal	[val]
fountain	fontein	[fontæjn]

allée (garden walkway)	laning	[laniŋ]
park	park	[park]
boulevard	boulevard	[bulefar]
square	plein	[plæjn]
avenue (wide street)	laan	[lān]
street	straat	[strāt]
side street	systraat	[saj·strāt]
dead end	doodloopstraat	[doədloəp·strāt]
house	huis	[hœis]
building	gebou	[χebæʊ]

skyscraper	**wolkekrabber**	[volkə·krabbər]
facade	**gewel**	[χevəl]
roof	**dak**	[dak]
window	**venster**	[fɛŋstər]
arch	**arkade**	[arkadə]
column	**kolom**	[kolom]
corner	**hoek**	[huk]
store window	**uitstalraam**	[œitstalrãm]
signboard (store sign, etc.)	**reklamebord**	[reklamə·bort]
poster	**plakkaat**	[plakkãt]
advertising poster	**reklameplakkaat**	[reklamə·plakkãt]
billboard	**aanplakbord**	[ãnplakbort]
garbage, trash	**vullis**	[fullis]
trashcan (public ~)	**vullisbak**	[fullis·bak]
to litter (vi)	**rommel strooi**	[rommǝl stroj]
garbage dump	**vullishoop**	[fullis·hoəp]
phone booth	**telefoonhokkie**	[telefoən·hokki]
lamppost	**lamppaal**	[lamp·pãl]
bench (park ~)	**bank**	[bank]
police officer	**polisieman**	[polisi·man]
police	**polisie**	[polisi]
beggar	**bedelaar**	[bedelãr]
homeless (n)	**daklose**	[daklosə]

76. Urban institutions

store	**winkel**	[vinkəl]
drugstore, pharmacy	**apteek**	[apteək]
eyeglass store	**optisiën**	[optisiɛn]
shopping mall	**winkelsentrum**	[vinkəl·sentrum]
supermarket	**supermark**	[supermark]
bakery	**bakkery**	[bakkeraj]
baker	**bakker**	[bakkər]
pastry shop	**banketbakkery**	[banket·bakkeraj]
grocery store	**kruidenierswinkel**	[krœidenirs·vinkəl]
butcher shop	**slagter**	[slaχtər]
produce store	**groentewinkel**	[χruntə·vinkəl]
market	**mark**	[mark]
coffee house	**koffiekroeg**	[koffi·kruχ]
restaurant	**restaurant**	[restourant]
pub, bar	**kroeg**	[kruχ]
pizzeria	**pizzeria**	[pizzeria]
hair salon	**haarsalon**	[hãr·salon]

post office	**poskantoor**	[pos·kantoər]
dry cleaners	**droogskoonmakers**	[droəχ·skoən·makers]
photo studio	**fotostudio**	[foto·studio]
shoe store	**skoenwinkel**	[skun·vinkəl]
bookstore	**boekhandel**	[buk·handəl]
sporting goods store	**sportwinkel**	[sport·vinkəl]
clothes repair shop	**klereherstelwinkel**	[klerə·herstəl·vinkəl]
formal wear rental	**klereverhuurwinkel**	[klerə·ferhɪr·vinkəl]
video rental store	**videowinkel**	[video·vinkəl]
circus	**sirkus**	[sirkus]
zoo	**dieretuin**	[dirə·tœin]
movie theater	**bioskoop**	[bioskoəp]
museum	**museum**	[musøəm]
library	**biblioteek**	[biblioteək]
theater	**teater**	[teatər]
opera (opera house)	**opera**	[opera]
nightclub	**nagklub**	[naχ·klup]
casino	**kasino**	[kasino]
mosque	**moskee**	[moskeə]
synagogue	**sinagoge**	[sinaχoχə]
cathedral	**katedraal**	[katedrãl]
temple	**tempel**	[tempəl]
church	**kerk**	[kerk]
college	**kollege**	[kolledʒ]
university	**universiteit**	[unifersitæjt]
school	**skool**	[skoəl]
prefecture	**stadhuis**	[stat·hœis]
city hall	**stadhuis**	[stat·hœis]
hotel	**hotel**	[hotəl]
bank	**bank**	[bank]
embassy	**ambassade**	[ambassadə]
travel agency	**reisagentskap**	[ræjs·aχentskap]
information office	**inligtingskantoor**	[inliχtiŋs·kantoər]
currency exchange	**wisselkantoor**	[vissəl·kantoər]
subway	**metro**	[metro]
hospital	**hospitaal**	[hospitãl]
gas station	**petrolstasie**	[petrol·stasi]
parking lot	**parkeerterrein**	[parkeər·terræjn]

77. Urban transportation

bus	**bus**	[bus]
streetcar	**trem**	[trem]
trolley bus	**trembus**	[trembus]
route (of bus, etc.)	**busroete**	[bus·rute]
number (e.g., bus ~)	**nommer**	[nommər]
to go by …	**ry per …**	[raj pər …]
to get on (~ the bus)	**inklim**	[inklim]
to get off …	**uitklim …**	[œitklim …]
stop (e.g., bus ~)	**halte**	[haltə]
next stop	**volgende halte**	[folχendə haltə]
terminus	**eindpunt**	[æjnd·punt]
schedule	**diensrooster**	[diŋs·roəstər]
to wait (vt)	**wag**	[vaχ]
ticket	**kaartjie**	[kārki]
fare	**reistarief**	[ræjs·tarif]
cashier (ticket seller)	**kaartjieverkoper**	[kārki·ferkopər]
ticket inspection	**kaartjiekontrole**	[kārki·kontrolə]
ticket inspector	**kontroleur**	[kontroløər]
to be late (for …)	**laat wees**	[lāt veəs]
to miss (~ the train, etc.)	**mis**	[mis]
to be in a hurry	**haastig wees**	[hāstəχ veəs]
taxi, cab	**taxi**	[taksi]
taxi driver	**taxibestuurder**	[taksi·bestɪrdər]
by taxi	**per taxi**	[pər taksi]
taxi stand	**taxistaanplek**	[taksi·stānplek]
traffic	**verkeer**	[ferkeər]
traffic jam	**verkeersknoop**	[ferkeərs·knoəp]
rush hour	**spitsuur**	[spits·ɪr]
to park (vi)	**parkeer**	[parkeər]
to park (vt)	**parkeer**	[parkeər]
parking lot	**parkeerterrein**	[parkeər·terræjn]
subway	**metro**	[metro]
station	**stasie**	[stasi]
to take the subway	**die metro vat**	[di metro fat]
train	**trein**	[træjn]
train station	**treinstasie**	[træjn·stasi]

78. Sightseeing

monument	**monument**	[monument]
fortress	**fort**	[fort]

palace	paleis	[palæjs]
castle	kasteel	[kasteəl]
tower	toring	[toriŋ]
mausoleum	mausoleum	[mɔusoløəm]

architecture	argitektuur	[arχitektɪr]
medieval (adj)	Middeleeus	[middeliʊs]
ancient (adj)	oud	[æʊt]
national (adj)	nasionaal	[naʃionãl]
famous (monument, etc.)	bekend	[bekent]

tourist	toeris	[turis]
guide (person)	gids	[χids]
excursion, sightseeing tour	uitstappie	[œitstappi]
to show (vt)	wys	[vajs]
to tell (vt)	vertel	[fertəl]

to find (vt)	vind	[fint]
to get lost (lose one's way)	verdwaal	[ferdwãl]
map (e.g., subway ~)	kaart	[kãrt]
map (e.g., city ~)	kaart	[kãrt]

souvenir, gift	aandenking	[ãndenkiŋ]
gift shop	geskenkwinkel	[χeskɛnk·vinkəl]
to take pictures	fotografeer	[fotoχrafeər]
to have one's picture taken	jou portret laat maak	[jæʊ portret lãt mãk]

79. Shopping

to buy (purchase)	koop	[koəp]
purchase	aankoop	[ãnkoəp]
to go shopping	inkopies doen	[inkopis dun]
shopping	inkoop	[inkoəp]

to be open (ab. store)	oop wees	[oəp veəs]
to be closed	toe wees	[tu veəs]

footwear, shoes	skoeisel	[skuisəl]
clothes, clothing	klere	[klerə]
cosmetics	kosmetika	[kosmetika]
food products	voedingsware	[fudiŋs·warə]
gift, present	present	[present]

salesman	verkoper	[ferkopər]
saleswoman	verkoopsdame	[ferkoəps·damə]

check out, cash desk	kassier	[kassir]
mirror	spieël	[spiɛl]
counter (store ~)	toonbank	[toən·bank]
fitting room	paskamer	[pas·kamər]

to try on	aanpas	[ānpas]
to fit (ab. dress, etc.)	pas	[pas]
to like (I like ...)	hou van	[hæʊ fan]

price	prys	[prajs]
price tag	pryskaartjie	[prajs·kārki]
to cost (vt)	kos	[kos]
How much?	Hoeveel?	[hufeəl?]
discount	afslag	[afslaχ]

inexpensive (adj)	billik	[billik]
cheap (adj)	goedkoop	[χudkoəp]
expensive (adj)	duur	[dɪr]
It's expensive	dis duur	[dis dɪr]

rental (n)	verhuur	[ferhɪr]
to rent (~ a tuxedo)	verhuur	[ferhɪr]
credit (trade credit)	krediet	[krediet]
on credit (adv)	op krediet	[op krediet]

80. Money

money	geld	[χɛlt]
currency exchange	valutaruil	[faluta·rœil]
exchange rate	wisselkoers	[vissəl·kurs]
ATM	OTM	[o·te·em]
coin	muntstuk	[muntstuk]

| dollar | dollar | [dollar] |
| euro | euro | [øəro] |

lira	lira	[lira]
Deutschmark	Duitse mark	[dœitsə mark]
franc	frank	[frank]
pound sterling	pond sterling	[pont sterliŋ]
yen	yen	[jɛn]

debt	skuld	[skult]
debtor	skuldenaar	[skuldenār]
to lend (money)	uitleen	[œitleən]
to borrow (vi, vt)	leen	[leən]

bank	bank	[bank]
account	rekening	[rekəniŋ]
to deposit (vt)	deponeer	[deponeər]
to withdraw (vt)	trek	[trek]

credit card	kredietkaart	[kredit·kārt]
cash	kontant	[kontant]
check	tjek	[tʃek]

checkbook	tjekboek	[tʃek·buk]
wallet	beursie	[bøərsi]
change purse	muntstukbeursie	[muntstuk·bøərsi]
safe	brandkas	[brant·kas]

heir	erfgenaam	[ɛrfχənām]
inheritance	erfenis	[ɛrfenis]
fortune (wealth)	fortuin	[fortœin]

lease	huur	[hɪr]
rent (money)	huur	[hɪr]
to rent (sth from sb)	huur	[hɪr]

price	prys	[prajs]
cost	prys	[prajs]
sum	som	[som]

to spend (vt)	spandeer	[spandeer]
expenses	onkoste	[onkostə]
to economize (vi, vt)	besuinig	[besœinəχ]
economical	ekonomies	[ɛkonomis]

to pay (vi, vt)	betaal	[betāl]
payment	betaling	[betaliŋ]
change (give the ~)	wisselgeld	[vissəl·χɛlt]

tax	belasting	[belastiŋ]
fine	boete	[butə]
to fine (vt)	beboet	[bebut]

81. Post. Postal service

post office	poskantoor	[pos·kantoər]
mail (letters, etc.)	pos	[pos]
mailman	posbode	[pos·bodə]
opening hours	besigheidsure	[besiχæjts·urə]

letter	brief	[brif]
registered letter	geregistreerde brief	[χereχistreərdə brif]
postcard	poskaart	[pos·kārt]
telegram	telegram	[teleχram]
package (parcel)	pakkie	[pakki]
money transfer	geldoorplasing	[χɛld·oərplasiŋ]

to receive (vt)	ontvang	[ontfaŋ]
to send (vt)	stuur	[stɪr]
sending	versending	[fersendiŋ]

| address | adres | [adres] |
| ZIP code | poskode | [pos·kodə] |

| sender | **sender** | [sendər] |
| receiver | **ontvanger** | [ontfaŋər] |

| name (first name) | **voornaam** | [foərnām] |
| surname (last name) | **van** | [fan] |

postage rate	**postarief**	[pos·tarif]
standard (adj)	**standaard**	[standārt]
economical (adj)	**ekonomies**	[ɛkonomis]

weight	**gewig**	[χevəχ]
to weigh (~ letters)	**weeg**	[veəχ]
envelope	**koevert**	[kufert]
postage stamp	**posseël**	[pos·seɛl]

Dwelling. House. Home

82. House. Dwelling

house	huis	[hœis]
at home (adv)	tuis	[tœis]
yard	werf	[verf]
fence (iron ~)	omheining	[omhæjniŋ]
brick (n)	baksteen	[baksteǝn]
brick (as adj)	baksteen-	[baksteǝn-]
stone (n)	klip	[klip]
stone (as adj)	klip-	[klip-]
concrete (n)	beton	[beton]
concrete (as adj)	beton-	[beton-]
new (new-built)	nuut	[nɪt]
old (adj)	ou	[æʊ]
decrepit (house)	vervalle	[ferfallǝ]
modern (adj)	moderne	[modernǝ]
multistory (adj)	multiverdieping-	[multi·ferdipiŋ-]
tall (~ building)	hoë	[hoɛ]
floor, story	verdieping	[ferdipiŋ]
single-story (adj)	enkelverdieping	[ɛnkǝl·ferdipiŋ]
1st floor	eerste verdieping	[eǝrstǝ ferdipiŋ]
top floor	boonste verdieping	[boǝŋstǝ verdipiŋ]
roof	dak	[dak]
chimney	skoorsteen	[skoǝrsteǝn]
roof tiles	dakteëls	[dakteɛls]
tiled (adj)	geteël	[χeteɛl]
attic (storage place)	solder	[soldǝr]
window	venster	[fɛŋstǝr]
glass	glas	[χlas]
window ledge	vensterbank	[fɛŋstǝr·bank]
shutters	luik	[lœik]
wall	muur	[mɪr]
balcony	balkon	[balkon]
downspout	reënpyp	[reɛn·pajp]
upstairs (to be ~)	bo	[bo]
to go upstairs	boontoe gaan	[boentu χãn]

to come down (the stairs)	afkom	[afkom]
to move (to new premises)	verhuis	[ferhœis]

83. House. Entrance. Lift

entrance	ingang	[inχaŋ]
stairs (stairway)	trap	[trap]
steps	treetjies	[treəkis]
banister	leuning	[løəniŋ]
lobby (hotel ~)	voorportaal	[foer·portāl]

mailbox	posbus	[pos·bus]
garbage can	vullisblik	[fullis·blik]
trash chute	vullisgeut	[fullis·χøət]

elevator	hysbak	[hajsbak]
freight elevator	vraghysbak	[fraχ·hajsbak]
elevator cage	hysbak	[hajsbak]
to take the elevator	hysbak neem	[hajsbak neəm]

apartment	woonstel	[voəŋstəl]
residents (~ of a building)	bewoners	[bevoners]
neighbor (masc.)	buurman	[bɪrman]
neighbor (fem.)	buurvrou	[bɪrfræʊ]
neighbors	bure	[burə]

84. House. Doors. Locks

door	deur	[døər]
gate (vehicle ~)	hek	[hɛk]
handle, doorknob	deurknop	[døər·knop]
to unlock (unbolt)	oopsluit	[oəpslœit]
to open (vt)	oopmaak	[oəpmāk]
to close (vt)	sluit	[slœit]

key	sleutel	[sløətəl]
bunch (of keys)	bos	[bos]
to creak (door, etc.)	kraak	[krāk]
creak	gekraak	[χekrāk]
hinge (door ~)	skarnier	[skarnir]
doormat	deurmat	[døər·mat]

door lock	deurslot	[døər·slot]
keyhole	sleutelgat	[sløətəl·χat]
crossbar (sliding bar)	grendel	[χrendəl]
door latch	deurknip	[døər·knip]
padlock	hangslot	[haŋslot]
to ring (~ the door bell)	lui	[lœi]

ringing (sound)	**gelui**	[χelœi]
doorbell	**deurklokkie**	[døər·klokki]
doorbell button	**belknoppie**	[bɛl·knoppi]
knock (at the door)	**klop**	[klop]
to knock (vi)	**klop**	[klop]
code	**kode**	[kodə]
combination lock	**kombinasieslot**	[kombinasi·slot]
intercom	**interkom**	[interkom]
number (on the door)	**nommer**	[nommər]
doorplate	**naambordjie**	[nãm·bordʒi]
peephole	**loergaatjie**	[lurχāki]

85. Country house

village	**dorp**	[dorp]
vegetable garden	**groentetuin**	[χruntə·tœin]
fence	**heining**	[hæjniŋ]
picket fence	**spitspaalheining**	[spitspāl·hæjniŋ]
wicket gate	**tuinhekkie**	[tœin·hɛkki]
granary	**graanstoorplek**	[χrāŋ·stoərplek]
root cellar	**wortelkelder**	[vortəl·keldər]
shed (garden ~)	**tuinhuisie**	[tœin·hœisi]
well (water)	**waterput**	[vatər·put]
stove (wood-fired ~)	**houtkaggel**	[hæʊt·kaχχəl]
to stoke the stove	**die houtkaggel stook**	[di hæʊt·kaχχəl stoək]
firewood	**brandhout**	[brant·hæʊt]
log (firewood)	**stomp**	[stomp]
veranda	**stoep**	[stup]
deck (terrace)	**dek**	[dek]
stoop (front steps)	**ingangstrappie**	[inχaŋs·trappi]
swing (hanging seat)	**swaai**	[swāi]

86. Castle. Palace

castle	**kasteel**	[kasteəl]
palace	**paleis**	[palæjs]
fortress	**fort**	[fort]
wall (round castle)	**ringmuur**	[riŋ·mɪr]
tower	**toring**	[toriŋ]
keep, donjon	**toring**	[toriŋ]
portcullis	**valhek**	[falhek]
underground passage	**tonnel**	[tonnəl]

moat	**grag**	[χraχ]
chain	**ketting**	[kɛttiŋ]
arrow loop	**skietgat**	[skitχat]
magnificent (adj)	**pragtig**	[praχtəχ]
majestic (adj)	**majestueus**	[majestuøəs]
impregnable (adj)	**onneembaar**	[onneəmbãr]
medieval (adj)	**Middeleeus**	[middeliʋs]

87. Apartment

apartment	**woonstel**	[voəŋstəl]
room	**kamer**	[kamər]
bedroom	**slaapkamer**	[slãp·kamər]
dining room	**eetkamer**	[eət·kamər]
living room	**sitkamer**	[sit·kamər]
study (home office)	**studeerkamer**	[studeər·kamər]
entry room	**ingangsportaal**	[inχaŋs·portãl]
bathroom (room with a bath or shower)	**badkamer**	[bad·kamər]
half bath	**toilet**	[tojlet]
ceiling	**plafon**	[plafon]
floor	**vloer**	[flur]
corner	**hoek**	[huk]

88. Apartment. Cleaning

to clean (vi, vt)	**skoonmaak**	[skoənmãk]
to put away (to stow)	**bère**	[bærə]
dust	**stof**	[stof]
dusty (adj)	**stoffig**	[stoffəχ]
to dust (vt)	**afstof**	[afstof]
vacuum cleaner	**stofsuier**	[stof·sœiər]
to vacuum (vt)	**stofsuig**	[stofsœiχ]
to sweep (vi, vt)	**vee**	[feə]
sweepings	**veegsel**	[feəχsəl]
order	**orde**	[ordə]
disorder, mess	**wanorde**	[vanordə]
mop	**mop**	[mop]
dust cloth	**stoflap**	[stoflap]
short broom	**kort besem**	[kort besem]
dustpan	**skoppie**	[skoppi]

89. Furniture. Interior

furniture	**meubels**	[møəbɛls]
table	**tafel**	[tafel]
chair	**stoel**	[stul]
bed	**bed**	[bet]
couch, sofa	**rusbank**	[rusbank]
armchair	**gemakstoel**	[χemak·stul]
bookcase	**boekkas**	[buk·kas]
shelf	**rak**	[rak]
wardrobe	**klerekas**	[klerə·kas]
coat rack (wall-mounted ~)	**kapstok**	[kapstok]
coat stand	**kapstok**	[kapstok]
bureau, dresser	**laaikas**	[lājkas]
coffee table	**koffietafel**	[koffi·tafəl]
mirror	**spieël**	[spiɛl]
carpet	**mat**	[mat]
rug, small carpet	**matjie**	[maki]
fireplace	**vuurherd**	[fɪr·hert]
candle	**kers**	[kers]
candlestick	**kandelaar**	[kandelār]
drapes	**gordyne**	[χordajnə]
wallpaper	**muurpapier**	[mɪr·papir]
blinds (jalousie)	**blindings**	[blindiŋs]
table lamp	**tafellamp**	[tafel·lamp]
wall lamp (sconce)	**muurlamp**	[mɪr·lamp]
floor lamp	**staanlamp**	[stān·lamp]
chandelier	**kroonlugter**	[kroən·luχtər]
leg (of chair, table)	**poot**	[poət]
armrest	**armleuning**	[arm·løəniŋ]
back (backrest)	**rugleuning**	[ruχ·løəniŋ]
drawer	**laai**	[lāi]

90. Bedding

bedclothes	**beddegoed**	[beddə·χut]
pillow	**kussing**	[kussiŋ]
pillowcase	**kussingsloop**	[kussiŋ·sloəp]
duvet, comforter	**duvet**	[dufet]
sheet	**laken**	[laken]
bedspread	**bedsprei**	[bed·spræj]

91. Kitchen

kitchen	kombuis	[kombœis]
gas	gas	[χas]
gas stove (range)	gasstoof	[χas·stoəf]
electric stove	elektriese stoof	[elektrisə stoəf]
oven	oond	[oent]
microwave oven	mikrogolfoond	[mikroχolf·oent]

refrigerator	yskas	[ajs·kas]
freezer	vrieskas	[friskas]
dishwasher	skottelgoedwasser	[skottɛlχud·wassər]

meat grinder	vleismeul	[flæjs·møəl]
juicer	versapper	[fersappər]
toaster	broodrooster	[broəd·roəstər]
mixer	menger	[meŋər]

coffee machine	koffiemasjien	[koffi·maʃin]
coffee pot	koffiepot	[koffi·pot]
coffee grinder	koffiemeul	[koffi·møəl]

kettle	fluitketel	[flœit·ketəl]
teapot	teepot	[teə·pot]
lid	deksel	[deksəl]
tea strainer	teesiffie	[teə·siffi]

spoon	lepel	[lepəl]
teaspoon	teelepeltjie	[teə·lepəlki]
soup spoon	soplepel	[sop·lepəl]
fork	vurk	[furk]
knife	mes	[mes]

tableware (dishes)	tafelgerei	[tafel·χeræj]
plate (dinner ~)	bord	[bort]
saucer	piering	[piriŋ]

shot glass	likeurglas	[likøər·χlas]
glass (tumbler)	glas	[χlas]
cup	koppie	[koppi]

sugar bowl	suikerpot	[sœikər·pot]
salt shaker	soutvaatjie	[sæut·fāki]
pepper shaker	pepervaatjie	[pepər·fāki]
butter dish	botterbakkie	[bottər·bakki]

stock pot (soup pot)	soppot	[sop·pot]
frying pan (skillet)	braaipan	[brāj·pan]
ladle	opskeplepel	[opskep·lepəl]
colander	vergiet	[ferχit]
tray (serving ~)	skinkbord	[skink·bort]

bottle	bottel	[bottəl]
jar (glass)	fles	[fles]
can	blikkie	[blikki]

bottle opener	botteloopmaker	[bottəl·oəpmakər]
can opener	blikoopmaker	[blik·oəpmakər]
corkscrew	kurktrekker	[kurk·trɛkkər]
filter	filter	[filtər]
to filter (vt)	filter	[filtər]

| trash, garbage (food waste, etc.) | vullis | [fullis] |
| trash can (kitchen ~) | vullisbak | [fullis·bak] |

92. Bathroom

bathroom	badkamer	[bad·kamər]
water	water	[vatər]
faucet	kraan	[krãn]
hot water	warme water	[varmə vatər]
cold water	koue water	[kæʊə vatər]

toothpaste	tandepasta	[tandə·pasta]
to brush one's teeth	tande borsel	[tandə borsəl]
toothbrush	tandeborsel	[tandə·borsəl]

to shave (vi)	skeer	[skeər]
shaving foam	skeerroom	[skeər·roəm]
razor	skeermes	[skeər·mes]

to wash (one's hands, etc.)	was	[vas]
to take a bath	bad	[bat]
shower	stort	[stort]
to take a shower	stort	[stort]
bathtub	bad	[bat]
toilet (toilet bowl)	toilet	[tojlet]
sink (washbasin)	wasbak	[vas·bak]

| soap | seep | [seəp] |
| soap dish | seepbakkie | [seəp·bakki] |

sponge	spons	[spoŋs]
shampoo	sjampoe	[ʃampu]
towel	handdoek	[handduk]
bathrobe	badjas	[batjas]

laundry (process)	was	[vas]
washing machine	wasmasjien	[vas·maʃin]
to do the laundry	die wasgoed was	[di vasχut vas]
laundry detergent	waspoeier	[vas·pujer]

93. Household appliances

TV set	**TV-stel**	[te·fe-stəl]
tape recorder	**bandspeler**	[band·spelər]
VCR (video recorder)	**videomasjien**	[video·maʃin]
radio	**radio**	[radio]
player (CD, MP3, etc.)	**speler**	[spelər]
video projector	**videoprojektor**	[video·projektor]
home movie theater	**tuisfliekteater**	[tœis·flik·teatər]
DVD player	**DVD-speler**	[de·fe·de-spelər]
amplifier	**versterker**	[fersterkər]
video game console	**videokonsole**	[video·kɔŋsolə]
video camera	**videokamera**	[video·kamera]
camera (photo)	**kamera**	[kamera]
digital camera	**digitale kamera**	[diχitalə kamera]
vacuum cleaner	**stofsuier**	[stof·sœiər]
iron (e.g., steam ~)	**strykyster**	[strajk·ajstər]
ironing board	**strykplank**	[strajk·plank]
telephone	**telefoon**	[telefoən]
cell phone	**selfoon**	[sɛlfoən]
typewriter	**tikmasjien**	[tik·maʃin]
sewing machine	**naaimasjien**	[naj·maʃin]
microphone	**mikrofoon**	[mikrofoən]
headphones	**koptelefoon**	[kop·telefoən]
remote control (TV)	**afstandsbeheer**	[afstands·beheər]
CD, compact disc	**CD**	[se·de]
cassette, tape	**kasset**	[kasset]
vinyl record	**plaat**	[plãt]

94. Repairs. Renovation

renovations	**opknapwerk**	[opknap·werk]
to renovate (vt)	**opknap**	[opknap]
to repair, to fix (vt)	**herstel**	[herstəl]
to put in order	**aan kant maak**	[ãn kant mãk]
to redo (do again)	**oordoen**	[oərdun]
paint	**verf**	[ferf]
to paint (~ a wall)	**verf**	[ferf]
house painter	**skilder**	[skildər]
paintbrush	**verfborsel**	[ferf·borsəl]
whitewash	**witkalk**	[vitkalk]
to whitewash (vt)	**wit**	[vit]

wallpaper	muurpapier	[mɪr·papir]
to wallpaper (vt)	behang	[behaŋ]
varnish	vernis	[fernis]
to varnish (vt)	vernis	[fernis]

95. Plumbing

water	water	[vatər]
hot water	warme water	[varmə vatər]
cold water	koue water	[kæʊə vatər]
faucet	kraan	[krãn]

drop (of water)	druppel	[druppəl]
to drip (vi)	drup	[drup]
to leak (ab. pipe)	lek	[lek]
leak (pipe ~)	lekkasie	[lɛkkasi]
puddle	poeletjie	[puləki]

pipe	pyp	[pajp]
valve (e.g., ball ~)	kraan	[krãn]
to be clogged up	verstop raak	[ferstop rãk]

tools	gereedskap	[χereədskap]
adjustable wrench	skroefsleutel	[skruf·sløətəl]
to unscrew (lid, filter, etc.)	losskroef	[losskruf]
to screw (tighten)	vasskroef	[fasskruf]

to unclog (vt)	oopmaak	[oəpmãk]
plumber	loodgieter	[loədχitər]
basement	kelder	[kɛldər]
sewerage (system)	riolering	[rioleriŋ]

96. Fire. Conflagration

fire (accident)	brand	[brant]
flame	vlam	[flam]
spark	vonk	[fonk]
smoke (from fire)	rook	[roək]
torch (flaming stick)	fakkel	[fakkel]
campfire	kampvuur	[kampfɪr]

gas, gasoline	petrol	[petrol]
kerosene (type of fuel)	kerosien	[kerosin]
flammable (adj)	ontvambaar	[ontfambãr]
explosive (adj)	ontplofbaar	[ontplofbãr]
NO SMOKING	ROOK VERBODE	[roək ferbodə]
safety	veiligheid	[fæjliχæjt]
danger	gevaar	[χefãr]

dangerous (adj)	gevaarlik	[χefārlik]
to catch fire	vlam vat	[flam fat]
explosion	ontploffing	[ontploffiŋ]
to set fire	aan die brand steek	[ān di brant steək]
arsonist	brandstigter	[brant·stiχtər]
arson	brandstigting	[brant·stiχtiŋ]

to blaze (vi)	brand	[brant]
to burn (be on fire)	brand	[brant]
to burn down	afbrand	[afbrant]

to call the fire department	die brandweer roep	[di brantveər rup]
firefighter, fireman	brandweerman	[brantveər·man]
fire truck	brandweerwa	[brantveər·wa]
fire department	brandweer	[brantveər]
fire truck ladder	brandweerwaleer	[brantveər·wa·leər]

fire hose	brandslang	[brant·slaŋ]
fire extinguisher	brandblusser	[brant·blussər]
helmet	helmet	[hɛlmet]
siren	sirene	[sirenə]

to cry (for help)	skreeu	[skriu]
to call for help	hulp roep	[hulp rup]
rescuer	redder	[rɛddər]
to rescue (vt)	red	[ret]

to arrive (vi)	aankom	[ānkom]
to extinguish (vt)	blus	[blus]
water	water	[vatər]
sand	sand	[sant]

ruins (destruction)	ruïnes	[ruïnes]
to collapse (building, etc.)	instort	[instort]
to fall down (vi)	val	[fal]
to cave in (ceiling, floor)	instort	[instort]

| piece of debris | brokstukke | [brokstukkə] |
| ash | as | [as] |

| to suffocate (die) | verstik | [ferstik] |
| to be killed (perish) | omkom | [omkom] |

HUMAN ACTIVITIES

Job. Business. Part 1

97. Banking

bank	**bank**	[bank]
branch (of bank, etc.)	**tak**	[tak]
bank clerk, consultant	**bankklerk**	[bank·klerk]
manager (director)	**bestuurder**	[bestɪrdər]
bank account	**bankrekening**	[bank·rekəniŋ]
account number	**rekeningnommer**	[rekəniŋ·nommər]
checking account	**tjekrekening**	[tʃek·rekəniŋ]
savings account	**spaarrekening**	[spār·rekəniŋ]
to close the account	**die rekening sluit**	[di rekəniŋ slœit]
to withdraw (vt)	**trek**	[trek]
deposit	**deposito**	[deposito]
wire transfer	**telegrafiese oorplasing**	[teleχrafisə oərplasiŋ]
to wire, to transfer	**oorplaas**	[oərplās]
sum	**som**	[som]
How much?	**Hoeveel?**	[hufeəl?]
signature	**handtekening**	[hand·tekəniŋ]
to sign (vt)	**onderteken**	[ondərtekən]
credit card	**kredietkaart**	[kredit·kārt]
code (PIN code)	**kode**	[kodə]
credit card number	**kredietkaartnommer**	[kredit·kārt·nommər]
ATM	**OTM**	[o·te·em]
check	**tjek**	[tʃek]
checkbook	**tjekboek**	[tʃek·buk]
loan (bank ~)	**lening**	[leniŋ]
guarantee	**waarborg**	[vārborχ]

98. Telephone. Phone conversation

telephone	**telefoon**	[telefoən]
cell phone	**selfoon**	[sɛlfoən]

answering machine	antwoordmasjien	[antwoərt·maʃin]
to call (by phone)	bel	[bəl]
phone call	oproep	[oprup]

Hello!	Hallo!	[hallo!]
to ask (vt)	vra	[fra]
to answer (vi, vt)	antwoord	[antwoərt]

to hear (vt)	hoor	[hoər]
well (adv)	goed	[χut]
not well (adv)	nie goed nie	[ni χut ni]
noises (interference)	steurings	[støəriŋs]

receiver	gehoorstuk	[χehoərstuk]
to pick up (~ the phone)	optel	[optəl]
to hang up (~ the phone)	afskakel	[afskakəl]

busy (engaged)	besig	[besəχ]
to ring (ab. phone)	lui	[lœi]
telephone book	telefoongids	[telefoən·χids]

local (adj)	lokale	[lokalə]
local call	lokale oproep	[lokalə oprup]
long distance (~ call)	langafstand	[lanχ·afstant]
long-distance call	langafstand oproep	[lanχ·afstant oprup]
international (adj)	internasionale	[internaʃionalə]
international call	internasionale oproep	[internaʃionalə oprup]

99. Cell phone

cell phone	selfoon	[sɛlfoən]
display	skerm	[skerm]
button	knoppie	[knoppi]
SIM card	SIMkaart	[sim·kãrt]

battery	battery	[battəraj]
to be dead (battery)	pap wees	[pap veəs]
charger	batterylaaier	[battəraj·lajer]

menu	spyskaart	[spajs·kãrt]
settings	instellings	[instɛlliŋs]
tune (melody)	wysie	[vajsi]
to select (vt)	kies	[kis]

calculator	sakrekenaar	[sakrekənãr]
voice mail	stempos	[stem·pos]
alarm clock	wekker	[vɛkkər]
contacts	kontakte	[kontaktə]
SMS (text message)	SMS	[es·em·es]
subscriber	intekenaar	[intekənãr]

100. Stationery

ballpoint pen	**bolpen**	[bol·pen]
fountain pen	**vulpen**	[ful·pen]
pencil	**potlood**	[potloət]
highlighter	**merkpen**	[merk·pen]
felt-tip pen	**viltpen**	[filt·pen]
notepad	**notaboekie**	[nota·buki]
agenda (diary)	**dagboek**	[daχ·buk]
ruler	**liniaal**	[liniāl]
calculator	**sakrekenaar**	[sakrekənār]
eraser	**uitveër**	[œitfeɛr]
thumbtack	**duimspyker**	[dœim·spajkər]
paper clip	**skuifspeld**	[skœif·spɛlt]
glue	**gom**	[χom]
stapler	**krammasjien**	[kram·maʃin]
hole punch	**ponsmasjien**	[poŋs·maʃin]
pencil sharpener	**skerpmaker**	[skerp·makər]

Job. Business. Part 2

101. Mass Media

newspaper	koerant	[kurant]
magazine	tydskrif	[tajdskrif]
press (printed media)	pers	[pers]
radio	radio	[radio]
radio station	omroep	[omrup]
television	televisie	[telefisi]

presenter, host	aanbieder	[ānbidər]
newscaster	nuusleser	[nɪslesər]
commentator	kommentator	[kommentator]

journalist	joernalis	[jurnalis]
correspondent (reporter)	korrespondent	[korrespondɛnt]
press photographer	persfotograaf	[pers·fotoχrāf]
reporter	verslaggewer	[ferslaχ·χevər]

editor	redakteur	[redaktøər]
editor-in-chief	hoofredakteur	[hoəf·redaktøər]

to subscribe (to …)	inteken op …	[intekən op …]
subscription	intekening	[intekəniŋ]
subscriber	intekenaar	[intekənār]
to read (vi, vt)	lees	[leəs]
reader	leser	[lesər]

circulation (of newspaper)	oplaag	[oplāχ]
monthly (adj)	maandeliks	[māndəliks]
weekly (adj)	weekliks	[veəkliks]
issue (edition)	nommer	[nommər]
new (~ issue)	nuwe	[nuvə]

headline	opskrif	[opskrif]
short article	kort artikel	[kort artikəl]
column (regular article)	kolom	[kolom]
article	artikel	[artikəl]
page	bladsy	[bladsaj]

reportage, report	veslag	[feslaχ]
event (happening)	gebeurtenis	[χebøərtenis]
sensation (news)	sensasie	[sɛŋsasi]
scandal	skandaal	[skandāl]
scandalous (adj)	skandelik	[skandəlik]

great (~ scandal)	groot	[ɣroet]
show (e.g., cooking ~)	program	[proɣram]
interview	onderhoud	[ondərhæʊt]
live broadcast	regstreekse uitsending	[reҳstreeksə œitsendiŋ]
channel	kanaal	[kanāl]

102. Agriculture

agriculture	landbou	[landbæʊ]
peasant (masc.)	boer	[bur]
peasant (fem.)	boervrou	[bur·fræʊ]
farmer	boer	[bur]
tractor (farm ~)	trekker	[trɛkkər]
combine, harvester	stroper	[stropər]
plow	ploeg	[pluҳ]
to plow (vi, vt)	ploeg	[pluҳ]
plowland	ploegland	[pluҳlant]
furrow (in field)	voor	[foər]
to sow (vi, vt)	saai	[sāi]
seeder	saaier	[sājer]
sowing (process)	saai	[sāi]
scythe	sens	[sɛŋs]
to mow, to scythe	maai	[māi]
spade (tool)	graaf	[ɣrāf]
to till (vt)	omspit	[omspit]
hoe	skoffel	[skoffəl]
to hoe, to weed	skoffel	[skoffəl]
weed (plant)	onkruid	[onkrœit]
watering can	gieter	[ɣitər]
to water (plants)	nat gooi	[nat ҳoj]
watering (act)	nat gooi	[nat ҳoj]
pitchfork	gaffel	[ҳaffəl]
rake	hark	[hark]
fertilizer	misstof	[misstof]
to fertilize (vt)	bemes	[bemes]
manure (fertilizer)	misstof	[misstof]
field	veld	[fɛlt]
meadow	weiland	[væjlant]
vegetable garden	groentetuin	[ҳruntə·tœin]
orchard (e.g., apple ~)	boord	[boərt]

to graze (vt)	wei	[væj]
herder (herdsman)	herder	[herdər]
pasture	weiland	[væjlant]

| cattle breeding | veeboerdery | [feə·burderaj] |
| sheep farming | skaapboerdery | [skāp·burderaj] |

plantation	aanplanting	[ānplantiŋ]
row (garden bed ~s)	bedding	[beddiŋ]
hothouse	broeikas	[bruikas]

| drought (lack of rain) | droogte | [droəχtə] |
| dry (~ summer) | droog | [droəχ] |

grain	graan	[χrān]
cereal crops	graangewasse	[χrān·χəwassə]
to harvest, to gather	oes	[us]

miller (person)	meulenaar	[møəlenār]
mill (e.g., gristmill)	meul	[møəl]
to grind (grain)	maal	[māl]
flour	meelblom	[meəl·blom]
straw	strooi	[stroj]

103. Building. Building process

construction site	bouperseel	[bæʊ·perseəl]
to build (vt)	bou	[bæʊ]
construction worker	bouwerker	[bæʊ·verkər]

project	projek	[projek]
architect	argitek	[arχitek]
worker	werker	[verkər]

foundation (of a building)	fondament	[fondament]
roof	dak	[dak]
foundation pile	heipaal	[hæjpāl]
wall	muur	[mɪr]

| reinforcing bars | betonstaal | [betɔŋ·stāl] |
| scaffolding | steiers | [stæjers] |

concrete	beton	[beton]
granite	graniet	[χranit]
stone	klip	[klip]
brick	baksteen	[baksteən]

sand	sand	[sant]
cement	sement	[sement]
plaster (for walls)	pleister	[plæjstər]

to plaster (vt)	**pleister**	[plæjstər]
paint	**verf**	[ferf]
to paint (~ a wall)	**verf**	[ferf]
barrel	**drom**	[drom]
crane	**kraan**	[krãn]
to lift, to hoist (vt)	**optel**	[optəl]
to lower (vt)	**laat sak**	[lãt sak]
bulldozer	**stootskraper**	[stoət·skrapər]
excavator	**graafmasjien**	[χrãf·maʃin]
scoop, bucket	**bak**	[bak]
to dig (excavate)	**grawe**	[χravə]
hard hat	**helmet**	[hɛlmet]

Professions and occupations

104. Job search. Dismissal

job	**baantjie**	[bānki]
staff (work force)	**personeel**	[personeəl]
personnel	**personeel**	[personeəl]
career	**loopbaan**	[loəpbān]
prospects (chances)	**vooruitsigte**	[foərœit·siχtə]
skills (mastery)	**meesterskap**	[meəsterskap]
selection (screening)	**seleksie**	[seleksi]
employment agency	**arbeidsburo**	[arbæjds·buro]
résumé	**curriculum vitae**	[kurrikulum fitaə]
job interview	**werksonderhoud**	[werk·ondərhæʊt]
vacancy, opening	**vakature**	[fakaturə]
salary, pay	**salaris**	[salaris]
fixed salary	**vaste salaris**	[fastə salaris]
pay, compensation	**loon**	[loən]
position (job)	**posisie**	[posisi]
duty (of employee)	**taak**	[tāk]
range of duties	**reeks opdragte**	[reəks opdraχtə]
busy (I'm ~)	**besig**	[besəχ]
to fire (dismiss)	**afdank**	[afdank]
dismissal	**afdanking**	[afdankiŋ]
unemployment	**werkloosheid**	[verkloəshæjt]
unemployed (n)	**werkloos**	[verkloəs]
retirement	**pensioen**	[pɛnsiun]
to retire (from job)	**met pensioen gaan**	[met pɛnsiun χān]

105. Business people

director	**direkteur**	[direktøər]
manager (director)	**bestuurder**	[bestɪrdər]
boss	**baas**	[bās]
superior	**hoof**	[hoəf]
superiors	**hoofde**	[hoəfdə]
president	**direkteur**	[direktøər]

chairman	voorsitter	[foərsittər]
deputy (substitute)	adjunk	[adjunk]
assistant	assistent	[assistent]
secretary	sekretaris	[sekretaris]
personal assistant	persoonlike assistent	[persoənlikə assistent]

businessman	sakeman	[sakəman]
entrepreneur	entrepreneur	[ɛntrəprenøər]
founder	stigter	[stiχtər]
to found (vt)	stig	[stiχ]

incorporator	stigter	[stiχtər]
partner	vennoot	[fɛnnoət]
stockholder	aandeelhouer	[āndeəl·hæʊər]

millionaire	miljoenêr	[miljunær]
billionaire	miljardêr	[miljardær]
owner, proprietor	eienaar	[æjenãr]
landowner	grondeienaar	[χront·æjenãr]

client	kliënt	[kliɛnt]
regular client	vaste kliënt	[fastə kliɛnt]
buyer (customer)	koper	[kopər]
visitor	besoeker	[besukər]

professional (n)	professioneel	[profɛssioneəl]
expert	kenner	[kɛnnər]
specialist	spesialis	[spesialis]

| banker | bankier | [bankir] |
| broker | makelaar | [makəlãr] |

cashier, teller	kassier	[kassir]
accountant	boekhouer	[bukhæʊər]
security guard	veiligheidswag	[fæjliχæjts·waχ]

investor	belegger	[beleχər]
debtor	skuldenaar	[skuldenãr]
creditor	krediteur	[kreditøər]
borrower	lener	[lenər]

| importer | invoerder | [infurdər] |
| exporter | uitvoerder | [œitfurdər] |

manufacturer	produsent	[produsent]
distributor	verdeler	[ferdelər]
middleman	tussenpersoon	[tussən·persoən]

consultant	raadgewer	[rãt·χevər]
sales representative	verkoopsagent	[ferkoəps·aχent]
agent	agent	[aχent]
insurance agent	versekeringsagent	[fersəkeriŋs·aχent]

106. Service professions

cook	**kok**	[kok]
chef (kitchen chef)	**sjef**	[ʃef]
baker	**bakker**	[bakkər]
bartender	**kroegman**	[kruχman]
waiter	**kelner**	[kɛlnər]
waitress	**kelnerin**	[kɛlnərin]
lawyer, attorney	**advokaat**	[adfokāt]
lawyer (legal expert)	**prokureur**	[prokurøər]
notary	**notaris**	[notaris]
electrician	**elektrisiën**	[ɛlektrisiɛn]
plumber	**loodgieter**	[loədχitər]
carpenter	**timmerman**	[timmerman]
masseur	**masseerder**	[masseərdər]
masseuse	**masseerster**	[masseərstər]
doctor	**dokter**	[doktər]
taxi driver	**taxibestuurder**	[taksi·bestɪrdər]
driver	**bestuurder**	[bestɪrdər]
delivery man	**koerier**	[kurir]
chambermaid	**kamermeisie**	[kamər·mæjsi]
security guard	**veiligheidswag**	[fæjliχæjts·waχ]
flight attendant (fem.)	**lugwaardin**	[luχ·wārdin]
schoolteacher	**onderwyser**	[ondərwajsər]
librarian	**bibliotekaris**	[bibliotekaris]
translator	**vertaler**	[fertalər]
interpreter	**tolk**	[tolk]
guide	**gids**	[χids]
hairdresser	**haarkapper**	[hār·kappər]
mailman	**posbode**	[pos·bodə]
salesman (store staff)	**verkoper**	[ferkopər]
gardener	**tuinman**	[tœin·man]
domestic servant	**bediende**	[bedində]
maid (female servant)	**bediende**	[bedində]
cleaner (cleaning lady)	**skoonmaakster**	[skoən·mākstər]

107. Military professions and ranks

private	**soldaat**	[soldāt]
sergeant	**sersant**	[sersant]

lieutenant	**luitenant**	[lœitənant]
captain	**kaptein**	[kaptæjn]
major	**majoor**	[majoər]
colonel	**kolonel**	[kolonəl]
general	**generaal**	[χenerāl]
marshal	**maarskalk**	[mārskalk]
admiral	**admiraal**	[admirāl]
military (n)	**leër**	[leɛr]
soldier	**soldaat**	[soldāt]
officer	**offisier**	[offisir]
commander	**kommandant**	[kommandant]
border guard	**grenswag**	[χrɛŋs·waχ]
radio operator	**radio-operateur**	[radio-operatøər]
scout (searcher)	**verkenner**	[ferkɛnnər]
pioneer (sapper)	**sappeur**	[sappøər]
marksman	**skutter**	[skuttər]
navigator	**navigator**	[nafiχator]

108. Officials. Priests

king	**koning**	[koniŋ]
queen	**koningin**	[koniŋin]
prince	**prins**	[prins]
princess	**prinses**	[prinsəs]
czar	**tsaar**	[tsār]
czarina	**tsarina**	[tsarina]
president	**president**	[president]
Secretary (minister)	**minister**	[ministər]
prime minister	**eerste minister**	[eərstə ministər]
senator	**senator**	[senator]
diplomat	**diplomaat**	[diplomāt]
consul	**konsul**	[kɔŋsul]
ambassador	**ambassadeur**	[ambassadøər]
counsilor (diplomatic officer)	**adviseur**	[adfisøər]
official, functionary (civil servant)	**amptenaar**	[amptənar]
prefect	**prefek**	[prefek]
mayor	**burgermeester**	[burgər·meəstər]
judge	**regter**	[reχtər]
prosecutor (e.g., district attorney)	**aanklaer**	[ānklaər]

missionary	sendeling	[sendəliŋ]
monk	monnik	[monnik]
abbot	ab	[ap]
rabbi	rabbi	[rabbi]
vizier	visier	[fisir]
shah	sjah	[ʃah]
sheikh	sjeik	[ʃæjk]

109. Agricultural professions

beekeeper	byeboer	[bajebur]
herder, shepherd	herder	[herdər]
agronomist	landboukundige	[landbæʊ·kundiχə]
cattle breeder	veeteler	[feə·telər]
veterinarian	veearts	[feə·arts]
farmer	boer	[bur]
winemaker	wynmaker	[vajn·makər]
zoologist	dierkundige	[dir·kundiχə]
cowboy	cowboy	[kovboj]

110. Art professions

actor	akteur	[aktøər]
actress	aktrise	[aktrisə]
singer (masc.)	sanger	[saŋər]
singer (fem.)	sangeres	[saŋəres]
dancer (masc.)	danser	[daŋsər]
dancer (fem.)	danseres	[daŋsərəs]
performer (masc.)	verhoogkunstenaar	[ferhoəχ·kunstənār]
performer (fem.)	verhoogkunstenares	[ferhoəχ·kunstənares]
musician	musikant	[musikant]
pianist	pianis	[pianis]
guitar player	kitaarspeler	[kitār·spelər]
conductor (orchestra ~)	dirigent	[diriχent]
composer	komponis	[komponis]
impresario	impresario	[impresario]
film director	filmregisseur	[film·reχissøər]
producer	produsent	[produsent]
scriptwriter	draaiboekskrywer	[drãjbuk·skrajvər]
critic	kritikus	[kritikus]

writer	**skrywer**	[skrajvər]
poet	**digter**	[diχtər]
sculptor	**beeldhouer**	[beəldhæʋər]
artist (painter)	**kunstenaar**	[kunstenãr]

juggler	**jongleur**	[jonχløər]
clown	**hanswors**	[haŋswors]
acrobat	**akrobaat**	[akrobãt]
magician	**goëlaar**	[χoɛlãr]

111. Various professions

doctor	**dokter**	[doktər]
nurse	**verpleegster**	[ferpleəχ·stər]
psychiatrist	**psigiater**	[psiχiatər]
dentist	**tandarts**	[tand·arts]
surgeon	**chirurg**	[ʃirurχ]

astronaut	**astronout**	[astronæʋt]
astronomer	**astronoom**	[astronoəm]
pilot	**piloot**	[piloət]

driver (of taxi, etc.)	**bestuurder**	[bestɪrdər]
engineer (train driver)	**treindrywer**	[træjn·drajvər]
mechanic	**werktuigkundige**	[verktœiχ·kundiχə]

miner	**mynwerker**	[majn·werkər]
worker	**werker**	[verkər]
locksmith	**slotmaker**	[slot·makər]
joiner (carpenter)	**skrynwerker**	[skrajn·werkər]
turner (lathe machine operator)	**draaibankwerker**	[drãjbank·werkər]
construction worker	**bouwerker**	[bæʋ·verkər]
welder	**sweiser**	[swæjsər]

professor (title)	**professor**	[profɛssor]
architect	**argitek**	[arχitek]
historian	**historikus**	[historikus]
scientist	**wetenskaplike**	[vetɛŋskaplikə]
physicist	**fisikus**	[fisikus]
chemist (scientist)	**skeikundige**	[skæjkundiχə]

archeologist	**argeoloog**	[arχeoloəχ]
geologist	**geoloog**	[χeoloəχ]
researcher (scientist)	**navorser**	[naforsər]

babysitter	**babasitter**	[babasittər]
teacher, educator	**onderwyser**	[ondərwajsər]
editor	**redakteur**	[redaktøər]
editor-in-chief	**hoofredakteur**	[hoəf·redaktøər]

correspondent	korrespondent	[korrespondɛnt]
typist (fem.)	tikster	[tikstər]

designer	ontwerper	[ontwerpər]
computer expert	rekenaarkenner	[rekənār·kɛnnər]
programmer	programmeur	[proχrammøər]
engineer (designer)	ingenieur	[inχeniøər]

sailor	matroos	[matroəs]
seaman	seeman	[seəman]
rescuer	redder	[rɛddər]

fireman	brandweerman	[brantveər·man]
police officer	polisieman	[polisi·man]
watchman	bewaker	[bevakər]
detective	speurder	[spøərdər]

customs officer	doeanebeampte	[duanə·beamptə]
bodyguard	lyfwag	[lajf·waχ]
prison guard	tronkbewaarder	[tronk·bevārdər]
inspector	inspekteur	[inspektøər]

sportsman	sportman	[sportman]
trainer, coach	breier	[bræjer]
butcher	slagter	[slaχtər]
cobbler (shoe repairer)	skoenmaker	[skun·makər]
merchant	handelaar	[handəlār]
loader (person)	laaier	[lājer]

fashion designer	modeontwerper	[modə·ontwerpər]
model (fem.)	model	[modəl]

112. Occupations. Social status

schoolboy	skoolseun	[skoəl·søən]
student (college ~)	student	[student]

philosopher	filosoof	[filosoəf]
economist	ekonoom	[ɛkonoəm]
inventor	uitvinder	[œitfindər]

unemployed (n)	werkloos	[verkloəs]
retiree	pensioentrekker	[pɛnsiun·trɛkkər]
spy, secret agent	spioen	[spiun]

prisoner	gevangene	[χefaŋənə]
striker	staker	[stakər]
bureaucrat	burokraat	[burokrāt]
traveler (globetrotter)	reisiger	[ræjsiχər]
gay, homosexual (n)	gay	[χaaj]

| hacker | **kuberkraker** | [kubər·krakər] |
| hippie | **hippie** | [hippi] |

bandit	**bandiet**	[bandit]
hit man, killer	**huurmoordenaar**	[hɪr·moərdenãr]
drug addict	**dwelmslaaf**	[dwɛlm·slãf]
drug dealer	**dwelmhandelaar**	[dwɛlm·handəlãr]
prostitute (fem.)	**prostituut**	[prostitɪt]
pimp	**pooier**	[pojer]

sorcerer	**towenaar**	[tovenãr]
sorceress (evil ~)	**heks**	[heks]
pirate	**piraat, seerower**	[pirãt], [seə·rovər]
slave	**slaaf**	[slãf]
samurai	**samoerai**	[samuraj]
savage (primitive)	**wilde**	[vildə]

Sports

113. Kinds of sports. Sportspersons

sportsman	**sportman**	[sportman]
kind of sports	**sportsoorte**	[sport·soərtə]
basketball	**basketbal**	[basketbal]
basketball player	**basketbalspeler**	[basketbal·spelər]
baseball	**bofbal**	[bofbal]
baseball player	**bofbalspeler**	[bofbal·spelər]
soccer	**sokker**	[sokkər]
soccer player	**sokkerspeler**	[sokkər·spelər]
goalkeeper	**doelwagter**	[dul·waχtər]
hockey	**hokkie**	[hokki]
hockey player	**hokkiespeler**	[hokki·spelər]
volleyball	**vlugbal**	[fluχbal]
volleyball player	**vlugbalspeler**	[fluχbal·spelər]
boxing	**boks**	[boks]
boxer	**bokser**	[boksər]
wrestling	**stoei**	[stui]
wrestler	**stoeier**	[stujer]
karate	**karate**	[karatə]
karate fighter	**karatevegter**	[karatə·feχtər]
judo	**judo**	[judo]
judo athlete	**judoka**	[judoka]
tennis	**tennis**	[tɛnnis]
tennis player	**tennisspeler**	[tɛnnis·spelər]
swimming	**swem**	[swem]
swimmer	**swemmer**	[swemmər]
fencing	**skerm**	[skerm]
fencer	**skermer**	[skermər]
chess	**skaak**	[skāk]
chess player	**skaakspeler**	[skāk·spelər]

| alpinism | alpinisme | [alpinismə] |
| alpinist | alpinis | [alpinis] |

| running | hardloop | [hardloəp] |
| runner | hardloper | [hardlopər] |

| athletics | atletiek | [atletik] |
| athlete | atleet | [atleət] |

| horseback riding | perdry | [perdraj] |
| horse rider | ruiter | [rœitər] |

figure skating	kunsskaats	[kuns·skāts]
figure skater (masc.)	kunsskaatser	[kuns·skātsər]
figure skater (fem.)	kunsskaatser	[kuns·skātsər]

| powerlifting | gewigoptel | [χeviχ·optəl] |
| powerlifter | gewigopteller | [χeviχ·optɛllər] |

| car racing | motorwedren | [motor·wedrən] |
| racing driver | renjaer | [renjaər] |

| cycling | fiets | [fits] |
| cyclist | fietser | [fitsər] |

broad jump	verspring	[fer·spriŋ]
pole vault	polsstokspring	[polsstok·spriŋ]
jumper	springer	[spriŋər]

114. Kinds of sports. Miscellaneous

football	sokker	[sokkər]
badminton	pluimbal	[plœimbal]
biathlon	tweekamp	[tweəkamp]
billiards	biljart	[biljart]

bobsled	bobslee	[bobsleə]
bodybuilding	liggaamsbou	[liχχāmsbæʊ]
water polo	waterpolo	[vatər·polo]
handball	handbal	[handbal]
golf	gholf	[golf]

rowing, crew	roei	[rui]
scuba diving	duik	[dœik]
cross-country skiing	veldski	[fɛlt·ski]
table tennis (ping-pong)	tafeltennis	[tafəl·tɛnnis]

sailing	seil	[sæjl]
rally racing	tydren jaag	[tajdren jāχ]
rugby	rugby	[ragbi]

| snowboarding | sneeuplankry | [sniʊ·plankraj] |
| archery | boogskiet | [boəχ·skit] |

115. Gym

| barbell | staafgewig | [stãf·χevəχ] |
| dumbbells | handgewigte | [hand·χeviχtə] |

training machine	oefenmasjien	[ufen·maʃin]
exercise bicycle	oefenfiets	[ufen·fits]
treadmill	trapmeul	[trapmøəl]

horizontal bar	rekstok	[rekstok]
parallel bars	brug	[bruχ]
vault (vaulting horse)	springperd	[spriŋ·pert]
mat (exercise ~)	oefenmat	[ufen·mat]

jump rope	springtou	[spriŋ·tæʊ]
aerobics	aërobiese oefeninge	[aɛrobisə ufeniŋə]
yoga	joga	[joga]

116. Sports. Miscellaneous

Olympic Games	Olimpiese Spele	[olimpisə spelə]
winner	oorwinnaar	[oərwinnãr]
to be winning	wen	[ven]
to win (vi)	wen	[ven]

| leader | leier | [læjer] |
| to lead (vi) | lei | [læj] |

first place	eerste plek	[eərstə plek]
second place	tweede plek	[tweədə plek]
third place	derde plek	[derdə plek]

medal	medalje	[medalje]
trophy	trofee	[trofeə]
prize cup (trophy)	beker	[bekər]
prize (in game)	prys	[prajs]
main prize	hoofprys	[hoəf·prajs]
record	rekord	[rekort]

| final | finale | [finalə] |
| final (adj) | finale | [finalə] |

champion	kampioen	[kampiun]
championship	kampioenskap	[kampiunskap]
stadium	stadion	[stadion]

stand (bleachers)	tribune	[tribunə]
fan, supporter	ondersteuner	[ondərstøənər]
opponent, rival	teëstander	[tɛstandər]
start (start line)	wegspringplek	[veχspriŋ·plek]
finish line	eindstreep	[æjnd·streəp]
defeat	nederlaag	[nedərlāχ]
to lose (not win)	verloor	[fɛrloər]
referee	skeidsregter	[skæjds·reχtər]
jury (judges)	beoordelaars	[be·oərdelārs]
score	stand	[stant]
tie	gelykspel	[χelajkspəl]
to tie (vi)	gelykop speel	[χelajkop speəl]
point	punt	[punt]
result (final score)	puntestand	[puntəstant]
period	periode	[periodə]
half-time	rustyd	[rustajt]
doping	opkikkers	[opkikkərs]
to penalize (vt)	straf	[straf]
to disqualify (vt)	diskwalifiseer	[diskwalifiseər]
apparatus	apparaat	[apparāt]
javelin	spies	[spis]
shot (metal ball)	koeël	[kuɛl]
ball (snooker, etc.)	bal	[bal]
aim (target)	doelwit	[dulwit]
target	teiken	[tæjkən]
to shoot (vi)	skiet	[skit]
accurate (~ shot)	akkuraat	[akkurāt]
trainer, coach	breier	[bræjer]
to train (sb)	afrig	[afrəχ]
to train (vi)	oefen	[ufen]
training	oefen	[ufen]
gym	gimnastieksaal	[χimnastik·sāl]
exercise (physical)	oefening	[ufeniŋ]
warm-up (athlete ~)	opwarm	[opwarm]

Education

117. School

school	**skool**	[skoəl]
principal (headmaster)	**prinsipaal**	[prinsipāl]
pupil (boy)	**leerder**	[leərdər]
pupil (girl)	**leerder**	[leərdər]
schoolboy	**skoolseun**	[skoəl·søən]
schoolgirl	**skooldogter**	[skoəl·doχtər]
to teach (sb)	**leer**	[leər]
to learn (language, etc.)	**leer**	[leər]
to learn by heart	**van buite leer**	[fan bœitə leər]
to learn (~ to count, etc.)	**leer**	[leər]
to be in school	**op skool wees**	[op skoəl veəs]
to go to school	**skooltoe gaan**	[skoəltu χān]
alphabet	**alfabet**	[alfabet]
subject (at school)	**vak**	[fak]
classroom	**klaskamer**	[klas·kamər]
lesson	**les**	[les]
recess	**pouse**	[pæʊsə]
school bell	**skoolbel**	[skoəl·bəl]
school desk	**skoolbank**	[skoəl·bank]
chalkboard	**bord**	[bort]
grade	**simbool**	[simboəl]
good grade	**goeie punt**	[χuje punt]
bad grade	**slegte punt**	[sleχtə punt]
mistake, error	**fout**	[fæʊt]
to make mistakes	**foute maak**	[fæʊtə māk]
to correct (an error)	**korrigeer**	[korriχeər]
cheat sheet	**afskryfbriefie**	[afskrajf·brifi]
homework	**huiswerk**	[hœis·werk]
exercise (in education)	**oefening**	[ufeniŋ]
to be present	**aanwesig wees**	[ānwesəχ veəs]
to be absent	**afwesig wees**	[afwesəχ veəs]
to miss school	**stokkies draai**	[stokkis drāj]
to punish (vt)	**straf**	[straf]

punishment	**straf**	[straf]
conduct (behavior)	**gedrag**	[χedraχ]
report card	**rapport**	[rapport]
pencil	**potlood**	[potloət]
eraser	**uitveër**	[œitfeɛr]
chalk	**kryt**	[krajt]
pencil case	**potloodsakkie**	[potloət·sakki]
schoolbag	**boekesak**	[bukə·sak]
pen	**pen**	[pen]
school notebook	**skryfboek**	[skrajf·buk]
textbook	**handboek**	[hand·buk]
compasses	**passer**	[passər]
to make technical drawings	**tegniese tekeninge maak**	[teχnisə tekənikə māk]
technical drawing	**tegniese tekening**	[teχnisə tekəniŋ]
poem	**gedig**	[χedəχ]
by heart (adv)	**van buite**	[fan bœitə]
to learn by heart	**van buite leer**	[fan bœitə leər]
school vacation	**skoolvakansie**	[skoəl·fakaŋsi]
to be on vacation	**met vakansie wees**	[met fakaŋsi veəs]
to spend one's vacation	**jou vakansie deurbring**	[jæʊ fakaŋsi døərbriŋ]
test (written math ~)	**toets**	[tuts]
essay (composition)	**opstel**	[opstəl]
dictation	**diktee**	[dikteə]
exam (examination)	**eksamen**	[ɛksamen]
experiment (e.g., chemistry ~)	**eksperiment**	[ɛksperiment]

118. College. University

academy	**akademie**	[akademi]
university	**universiteit**	[unifersitæjt]
faculty (e.g., ~ of Medicine)	**fakulteit**	[fakultæjt]
student (masc.)	**student**	[student]
student (fem.)	**student**	[student]
lecturer (teacher)	**lektor**	[lektor]
lecture hall, room	**lesingsaal**	[lesiŋ·sāl]
graduate	**gegradueerde**	[χeχradueərdə]
diploma	**sertifikaat**	[sertifikāt]
dissertation	**proefskrif**	[prufskrif]
study (report)	**navorsing**	[naforsiŋ]

laboratory	**laboratorium**	[laboratorium]
lecture	**lesing**	[lesiŋ]
coursemate	**medestudent**	[medə·student]
scholarship	**beurs**	[bøərs]
academic degree	**akademiese graad**	[akademisə χrāt]

119. Sciences. Disciplines

mathematics	**wiskunde**	[viskundə]
algebra	**algebra**	[alχebra]
geometry	**meetkunde**	[meətkundə]

astronomy	**astronomie**	[astronomi]
biology	**biologie**	[bioloχi]
geography	**geografie**	[χeoχrafi]
geology	**geologie**	[χeoloχi]
history	**geskiedenis**	[χeskidenis]

medicine	**geneeskunde**	[χeneəs·kundə]
pedagogy	**pedagogie**	[pedaχoχi]
law	**regte**	[reχtə]

physics	**fisika**	[fisika]
chemistry	**chemie**	[χemi]
philosophy	**filosofie**	[filosofi]
psychology	**sielkunde**	[silkundə]

120. Writing system. Orthography

grammar	**grammatika**	[χrammatika]
vocabulary	**woordeskat**	[voərdeskat]
phonetics	**fonetika**	[fonetika]

| noun | **selfstandige naamwoord** | [sɛlfstandiχə nāmwoərt] |
| adjective | **byvoeglike naamwoord** | [bajfuχlikə nāmvoərt] |

| verb | **werkwoord** | [verk·woərt] |
| adverb | **bijwoord** | [bij·woərt] |

pronoun	**voornaamwoord**	[foərnām·voərt]
interjection	**tussenwerpsel**	[tussən·werpsəl]
preposition	**voorsetsel**	[foərsetsəl]

root	**stam**	[stam]
ending	**agtervoegsel**	[aχtər·fuχsəl]
prefix	**voorvoegsel**	[foər·fuχsəl]
syllable	**lettergreep**	[lɛttər·χreəp]
suffix	**agtervoegsel, suffiks**	[aχtər·fuχsəl], [suffiks]

stress mark	klemteken	[klem·tekən]
apostrophe	afkappingsteken	[afkappiŋs·tekən]
period, dot	punt	[punt]
comma	komma	[komma]
semicolon	kommapunt	[komma·punt]

| colon | dubbelpunt | [dubbəl·punt] |
| ellipsis | beletselteken | [beletsəl·tekən] |

| question mark | vraagteken | [frãχ·tekən] |
| exclamation point | uitroepteken | [œitrup·tekən] |

| quotation marks | aanhalingstekens | [ãnhaliŋs·tekəŋs] |
| in quotation marks | tussen aanhalingstekens | [tussən ãnhaliŋs·tekəŋs] |

| parenthesis | hakies | [hakis] |
| in parenthesis | tussen hakies | [tussən hakis] |

hyphen	koppelteken	[koppəl·tekən]
dash	strepie	[strepi]
space (between words)	spasie	[spasi]

| letter | letter | [lɛttər] |
| capital letter | hoofletter | [hoəf·lɛttər] |

| vowel (n) | klinker | [klinkər] |
| consonant (n) | konsonant | [kɔŋsonant] |

sentence	sin	[sin]
subject	onderwerp	[ondərwerp]
predicate	predikaat	[predikãt]

| line | reël | [reɛl] |
| paragraph | paragraaf | [paraχrãf] |

word	woord	[voərt]
group of words	woordgroep	[voərt·χrup]
expression	uitdrukking	[œitdrukkiŋ]

| synonym | sinoniem | [sinonim] |
| antonym | antoniem | [antonim] |

rule	reël	[reɛl]
exception	uitsondering	[œitsondəriŋ]
correct (adj)	korrek	[korrek]

conjugation	vervoeging	[ferfuχiŋ]
declension	verbuiging	[ferbœəχiŋ]
nominal case	naamval	[nãmfal]
question	vraag	[frãχ]
to underline (vt)	onderstreep	[ondərstreəp]
dotted line	stippellyn	[stippəl·lajn]

121. Foreign languages

language	**taal**	[tāl]
foreign (adj)	**vreemd**	[freəmt]
foreign language	**vreemde taal**	[freəmdə tāl]
to study (vt)	**studeer**	[studeər]
to learn (language, etc.)	**leer**	[leər]

to read (vi, vt)	**lees**	[leəs]
to speak (vi, vt)	**praat**	[prāt]
to understand (vt)	**verstaan**	[ferstān]
to write (vt)	**skryf**	[skrajf]

fast (adv)	**vinnig**	[finnəχ]
slowly (adv)	**stadig**	[stadəχ]
fluently (adv)	**vlot**	[flot]

rules	**reëls**	[reɛls]
grammar	**grammatika**	[χrammatika]
vocabulary	**woordeskat**	[voərdeskat]
phonetics	**fonetika**	[fonetika]

textbook	**handboek**	[hand·buk]
dictionary	**woordeboek**	[voərdə·buk]
teach-yourself book	**selfstudie boek**	[sɛlfstudi buk]
phrasebook	**taalgids**	[tāl·χids]

cassette, tape	**kasset**	[kasset]
videotape	**videoband**	[video·bant]
CD, compact disc	**CD**	[se·de]
DVD	**DVD**	[de·fe·de]

alphabet	**alfabet**	[alfabet]
to spell (vt)	**spel**	[spel]
pronunciation	**uitspraak**	[œitsprāk]
accent	**aksent**	[aksent]

word	**woord**	[voərt]
meaning	**betekenis**	[betekənis]

course (e.g., a French ~)	**kursus**	[kursus]
to sign up	**inskryf**	[inskrajf]
teacher	**onderwyser**	[ondərwajsər]

translation (process)	**vertaling**	[fertaliŋ]
translation (text, etc.)	**vertaling**	[fertaliŋ]
translator	**vertaler**	[fertalər]
interpreter	**tolk**	[tolk]

polyglot	**poliglot**	[poliχlot]
memory	**geheue**	[χəhøə]

122. Fairy tale characters

Santa Claus	Kersvader	[kers·fadər]
Cinderella	Assepoester	[assepustər]
mermaid	meermin	[meərmin]
Neptune	Neptunus	[neptunus]
magician, wizard	towenaar	[tovenãr]
fairy	feetjie	[feəki]
magic (adj)	magies	[maχis]
magic wand	towerstaf	[tovər·staf]
fairy tale	sprokie	[sproki]
miracle	wonderwerk	[vondərwerk]
dwarf	dwerg	[dwerχ]
to turn into …	verander in …	[ferandər in …]
ghost	gees	[χeəs]
phantom	spook	[spoək]
monster	monster	[moŋstər]
dragon	draak	[drãk]
giant	reus	[røəs]

123. Zodiac Signs

Aries	Ram	[ram]
Taurus	Stier	[stir]
Gemini	Tweelinge	[tweəliŋə]
Cancer	Kreef	[kreəf]
Leo	Leeu	[liʊ]
Virgo	Maagd	[mãχt]
Libra	Weegskaal	[veəχskãl]
Scorpio	Skerpioen	[skerpiun]
Sagittarius	Boogskutter	[boəχskuttər]
Capricorn	Steenbok	[steənbok]
Aquarius	Waterman	[vatərman]
Pisces	Visse	[fissə]
character	karakter	[karaktər]
character traits	karaktertrekke	[karaktər·trɛkkə]
behavior	gedrag	[χedraχ]
to tell fortunes	waarsê	[vãrsɛ:]
fortune-teller	waarsêer	[vãrsɛər]
horoscope	horoskoop	[horoskoəp]

Arts

124. Theater

theater	teater	[teatər]
opera	opera	[opera]
operetta	operette	[operɛttə]
ballet	ballet	[ballet]
theater poster	plakkaat	[plakkāt]
troupe (theatrical company)	teatergeselskap	[teatər·ӽesɛlskap]
tour	toer	[tur]
to be on tour	op toer wees	[op tur veəs]
to rehearse (vi, vt)	repeteer	[repeteər]
rehearsal	repetisie	[repetisi]
repertoire	repertoire	[repertuarə]
performance	voorstelling	[foərstɛlliŋ]
theatrical show	opvoering	[opfuriŋ]
play	toneelstuk	[toneəl·stuk]
ticket	kaartjie	[kārki]
box office (ticket booth)	loket	[lokət]
lobby, foyer	voorportaal	[foər·portāl]
coat check (cloakroom)	bewaarkamer	[bevār·kamər]
coat check tag	bewaarkamerkaartjie	[bevār·kamər·kārki]
binoculars	verkyker	[ferkajkər]
usher	plekaanwyser	[plek·ānwajsər]
orchestra seats	stalles	[stalles]
balcony	balkon	[balkon]
dress circle	eerste balkon	[eərstə balkon]
box	losie	[losi]
row	ry	[raj]
seat	sitplek	[sitplek]
audience	gehoor	[ӽehoər]
spectator	toehoorders	[tuhoərders]
to clap (vi, vt)	klap	[klap]
applause	applous	[applæʊs]
ovation	toejuiging	[tujœəəӽiŋ]
stage	verhoog	[ferhoəӽ]
curtain	gordyn	[ӽordajn]
scenery	dekor	[dekor]

backstage	agter die verhoog	[aχtər di ferhoəχ]
scene (e.g., the last ~)	toneel	[toneəl]
act	bedryf	[bedrajf]
intermission	pouse	[pæusə]

125. Cinema

actor	akteur	[aktøər]
actress	aktrise	[aktrisə]

movies (industry)	filmbedryf	[film·bedrajf]
movie	fliek	[flik]
episode	episode	[ɛpisodə]

detective movie	speurfliek	[spøər·flik]
action movie	aksiefliek	[aksi·flik]
adventure movie	avontuurfliek	[afontrr·flik]
science fiction movie	wetenskapfiksiefilm	[vetɛŋskapfiksi·film]
horror movie	gruwelfliek	[χruvɛl·flik]

comedy movie	komedie	[komedi]
melodrama	melodrama	[melodrama]
drama	drama	[drama]

fictional movie	rolprent	[rolprent]
documentary	dokumentêre rolprent	[dokumentɛrə rolprent]
cartoon	tekenfilm	[tekən·film]
silent movies	stilprent	[stil·prent]

role (part)	rol	[rol]
leading role	hoofrol	[hoəf·rol]
to play (vi, vt)	speel	[speəl]

movie star	filmster	[film·stər]
well-known (adj)	bekend	[bekent]
famous (adj)	beroemd	[berumt]
popular (adj)	gewild	[χevilt]

script (screenplay)	draaiboek	[drãjbuk]
scriptwriter	draaiboekskrywer	[drãjbuk·skrajvər]
movie director	filmregisseur	[film·reχissøər]
producer	produsent	[produsent]
assistant	assistent	[assistent]
cameraman	kameraman	[kameraman]
stuntman	waaghals	[vãχhals]
double (stuntman)	dubbel	[dubbəl]

audition, screen test	filmtoets	[film·tuts]
shooting	skiet	[skit]
movie crew	filmspan	[film·span]

| movie set | rolprentstel | [rolprent·stəl] |
| camera | kamera | [kamera] |

| movie theater | bioskoop | [bioskoəp] |
| screen (e.g., big ~) | skerm | [skerm] |

soundtrack	klankbaan	[klank·bān]
special effects	spesiale effekte	[spesialə ɛffektə]
subtitles	onderskrif	[ondərskrif]
credits	erkenning	[ɛrkɛniŋ]
translation	vertaling	[fertaliŋ]

126. Painting

art	kuns	[kuns]
fine arts	skone kunste	[skonə kunstə]
art gallery	kunsgalery	[kuns·χaleraj]
art exhibition	kunsuitstalling	[kuns·œitstalliŋ]

painting (art)	skildery	[skilderaj]
graphic art	grafiese kuns	[χrafisə kuns]
abstract art	abstrakte kuns	[abstraktə kuns]
impressionism	impressionisme	[imprɛssionismə]

picture (painting)	skildery	[skilderaj]
drawing	tekening	[tekəniŋ]
poster	plakkaat	[plakkāt]

illustration (picture)	illustrasie	[illustrasi]
miniature	miniatuur	[miniatɪr]
copy (of painting, etc.)	kopie	[kopi]
reproduction	reproduksie	[reproduksi]

mosaic	mosaiek	[mosajek]
stained glass window	gebrandskilderde venster	[χebrandskilderdə fɛŋstər]
fresco	fresko	[fresko]
engraving	gravure	[χrafurə]

bust (sculpture)	borsbeeld	[borsbeəlt]
sculpture	beeldhouwerk	[beəldhæʊverk]
statue	standbeeld	[standbeəlt]
plaster of Paris	gips	[χips]
plaster (as adj)	gips-	[χips-]

portrait	portret	[portret]
self-portrait	selfportret	[sɛlf·portret]
landscape painting	landskap	[landskap]
still life	stillewe	[stilləvə]
caricature	karikatuur	[karikatɪr]

sketch	skets	[skets]
paint	verf	[ferf]
watercolor paint	waterverf	[vatər·ferf]
oil (paint)	olieverf	[oli·ferf]
pencil	potlood	[potloət]
India ink	Indiese ink	[indisə ink]
charcoal	houtskool	[hæʊts·koəl]

| to draw (vi, vt) | teken | [tekən] |
| to paint (vi, vt) | skilder | [skildər] |

to pose (vi)	poseer	[poseər]
artist's model (masc.)	naakmodel	[nākmodəl]
artist's model (fem.)	naakmodel	[nākmodəl]

artist (painter)	kunstenaar	[kunstenār]
work of art	kunswerk	[kuns·werk]
masterpiece	meesterstuk	[meestər·stuk]
studio (artist's workroom)	studio	[studio]

canvas (cloth)	doek	[duk]
easel	skildersesel	[skilders·esəl]
palette	palet	[palet]

frame (picture ~, etc.)	raam	[rām]
restoration	restourasie	[restæʊrasi]
to restore (vt)	restoureer	[restæʊreər]

127. Literature & Poetry

literature	literatuur	[literatɪr]
author (writer)	skrywer	[skrajvər]
pseudonym	skuilnaam	[skœil·nām]

book	boek	[buk]
volume	deel	[deəl]
table of contents	inhoudsopgawe	[inhæʊds·opχavə]
page	bladsy	[bladsaj]
main character	hoofkarakter	[hoəf·karaktər]
autograph	outograaf	[æʊtoχrāf]

short story	kortverhaal	[kort·ferhāl]
story (novella)	novelle	[nofɛllə]
novel	roman	[roman]
work (writing)	werk	[verk]
fable	fabel	[fabəl]
detective novel	speurroman	[spøər·roman]

| poem (verse) | gedig | [χedəχ] |
| poetry | digkuns | [diχkuns] |

poem (epic, ballad)	epos	[ɛpos]
poet	digter	[diχtər]

fiction	fiksie	[fiksi]
science fiction	wetenskapsfiksie	[vetɛŋskaps·fiksi]
adventures	avonture	[afonturə]
educational literature	opvoedkundige literatuur	[opfutkundiχə literatɪr]
children's literature	kinderliteratuur	[kindər·literatɪr]

128. Circus

circus	sirkus	[sirkus]
traveling circus	rondreisende sirkus	[rondræjsendə sirkus]
program	program	[proχram]
performance	voorstelling	[foərstɛliŋ]

act (circus ~)	nommer	[nommər]
circus ring	sirkusring	[sirkus·riŋ]

pantomime (act)	pantomime	[pantomimə]
clown	hanswors	[haŋswors]

acrobat	akrobaat	[akrobãt]
acrobatics	akrobatiek	[akrobatik]
gymnast	gimnas	[χimnas]
gymnastics	gimnastiek	[χimnastik]
somersault	salto	[salto]

athlete (strongman)	atleet	[atleət]
tamer (e.g., lion ~)	temmer	[tɛmmər]
rider (circus horse ~)	ruiter	[rœitər]
assistant	assistent	[assistent]

stunt	waaghalsige toertjie	[vãχhalsiχə turki]
magic trick	goëltoertjie	[χoɛl·turki]
conjurer, magician	goëlaar	[χoɛlãr]

juggler	jongleur	[jonχløər]
to juggle (vi, vt)	jongleer	[jonχleər]
animal trainer	dresseerder	[drɛsseər·dər]
animal training	dressering	[drɛsseriŋ]
to train (animals)	afrig	[afrəχ]

129. Music. Pop music

music	musiek	[musik]
musician	musikant	[musikant]

| musical instrument | musiekinstrument | [musik·instrument] |
| to play … | speel … | [speəl …] |

guitar	kitaar	[kitãr]
violin	viool	[fioəl]
cello	tjello	[ʧello]
double bass	kontrabas	[kontrabas]
harp	harp	[harp]

piano	piano	[piano]
grand piano	vleuelklavier	[fløɛl·klafir]
organ	orrel	[orrəl]

wind instruments	blaasinstrumente	[blãs·instrumentə]
oboe	hobo	[hobo]
saxophone	saksofoon	[saksofoən]
clarinet	klarinet	[klarinet]
flute	dwarsfluit	[dwars·flœit]
trumpet	trompet	[trompet]

accordion	trekklavier	[trɛkklafir]
drum	trommel	[tromməl]
duo	duet	[duet]
trio	trio	[trio]
quartet	kwartet	[kwartet]
choir	koor	[koər]
orchestra	orkes	[orkes]

pop music	popmusiek	[pop·musik]
rock music	rockmusiek	[rok·musik]
rock group	rockgroep	[rok·χrup]
jazz	jazz	[jazz]

| idol | held | [hɛlt] |
| admirer, fan | bewonderaar | [bevonderãr] |

concert	konsert	[koŋsert]
symphony	simfonie	[simfoni]
composition	komposisie	[komposisi]
to compose (write)	komponeer	[komponeər]

singing (n)	sang	[saŋ]
song	lied	[lit]
tune (melody)	wysie	[vajsi]
rhythm	ritme	[ritmə]
blues	blues	[blues]

sheet music	bladmusiek	[blad·musik]
baton	dirigeerstok	[diriχeər·stok]
bow	strykstok	[strajk·stok]
string	snaar	[snãr]
case (e.g., guitar ~)	houer	[hæʋər]

Rest. Entertainment. Travel

130. Trip. Travel

tourism, travel	**toerisme**	[turismə]
tourist	**toeris**	[turis]
trip, voyage	**reis**	[ræjs]
adventure	**avontuur**	[afontɪr]
trip, journey	**reis**	[ræjs]
vacation	**vakansie**	[fakaŋsi]
to be on vacation	**met vakansie wees**	[met fakaŋsi veəs]
rest	**rus**	[rus]
train	**trein**	[træjn]
by train	**per trein**	[pər træjn]
airplane	**vliegtuig**	[fliχtœiχ]
by airplane	**per vliegtuig**	[pər fliχtœiχ]
by car	**per motor**	[pər motor]
by ship	**per skip**	[pər skip]
luggage	**bagasie**	[baχasi]
suitcase	**tas**	[tas]
luggage cart	**bagasiekarretjie**	[baχasi·karrəki]
passport	**paspoort**	[paspoərt]
visa	**visum**	[fisum]
ticket	**kaartjie**	[kārki]
air ticket	**lugkaartjie**	[luχ·kārki]
guidebook	**reisgids**	[ræjsχids]
map (tourist ~)	**kaart**	[kārt]
area (rural ~)	**gebied**	[χebit]
place, site	**plek**	[plek]
exotica (n)	**eksotiese dinge**	[ɛksotisə diŋə]
exotic (adj)	**eksoties**	[ɛksotis]
amazing (adj)	**verbasend**	[ferbasent]
group	**groep**	[χrup]
excursion, sightseeing tour	**uitstappie**	[œitstappi]
guide (person)	**gids**	[χids]

131. Hotel

hotel	**hotel**	[hotəl]
motel	**motel**	[motəl]
three-star (~ hotel)	**drie-ster**	[dri-stər]
five-star	**vyf-ster**	[fajf-stər]
to stay (in a hotel, etc.)	**oornag**	[oərnaχ]
room	**kamer**	[kamər]
single room	**enkelkamer**	[ɛnkəl·kamər]
double room	**dubbelkamer**	[dubbəl·kamər]
half board	**met aandete,**	[met āndetə],
	bed en ontbyt	[bet en ontbajt]
full board	**volle losies**	[follə losis]
with bath	**met bad**	[met bat]
with shower	**met stortbad**	[met stort·bat]
satellite television	**satelliet-TV**	[satɛllit-te·fe]
air-conditioner	**lugversorger**	[luχfersorχər]
towel	**handdoek**	[handduk]
key	**sleutel**	[sløətəl]
administrator	**bestuurder**	[bestɪrdər]
chambermaid	**kamermeisie**	[kamər·mæjsi]
porter, bellboy	**hoteljoggie**	[hotəl·joχi]
doorman	**portier**	[portir]
restaurant	**restaurant**	[restourant]
pub, bar	**kroeg**	[kruχ]
breakfast	**ontbyt**	[ontbajt]
dinner	**aandete**	[āndetə]
buffet	**buffetete**	[buffetetə]
lobby	**voorportaal**	[foər·portāl]
elevator	**hysbak**	[hajsbak]
DO NOT DISTURB	**MOENIE STEUR NIE**	[muni støər ni]
NO SMOKING	**ROOK VERBODE**	[roək ferbodə]

132. Books. Reading

book	**boek**	[buk]
author	**outeur**	[æʊtøər]
writer	**skrywer**	[skrajvər]
to write (~ a book)	**skryf**	[skrajf]
reader	**leser**	[lesər]
to read (vi, vt)	**lees**	[leəs]

reading (activity)	**lees**	[leəs]
silently (to oneself)	**stil**	[stil]
aloud (adv)	**hardop**	[hardop]
to publish (vt)	**uitgee**	[œitχeə]
publishing (process)	**uitgee**	[œitχeə]
publisher	**uitgewer**	[œitχevər]
publishing house	**uitgewery**	[œitχevəraj]
to come out (be released)	**verskyn**	[ferskajn]
release (of a book)	**verskyn**	[ferskajn]
print run	**oplaag**	[oplāχ]
bookstore	**boekhandel**	[buk·handəl]
library	**biblioteek**	[biblioteək]
story (novella)	**novelle**	[nofɛllə]
short story	**kortverhaal**	[kort·ferhāl]
novel	**roman**	[roman]
detective novel	**speurroman**	[spøər·roman]
memoirs	**memoires**	[memuares]
legend	**legende**	[leχendə]
myth	**mite**	[mitə]
poetry, poems	**poësie**	[poɛsi]
autobiography	**outobiografie**	[æʊtobioχrafi]
selected works	**bloemlesing**	[blumlesiŋ]
science fiction	**wetenskapsfiksie**	[vetɛŋskaps·fiksi]
title	**titel**	[titel]
introduction	**inleiding**	[inlæjdiŋ]
title page	**titelblad**	[titel·blat]
chapter	**hoofstuk**	[hoəfstuk]
extract	**fragment**	[fraχment]
episode	**episode**	[ɛpisodə]
plot (storyline)	**plot**	[plot]
contents	**inhoud**	[inhæʊt]
table of contents	**inhoudsopgawe**	[inhæʊds·opχavə]
main character	**hoofkarakter**	[hoəf·karaktər]
volume	**deel**	[deəl]
cover	**omslag**	[omslaχ]
binding	**band**	[bant]
bookmark	**bladwyser**	[blat·vajsər]
page	**bladsy**	[bladsaj]
to page through	**deurblaai**	[døərblāi]
margins	**marges**	[marχəs]
annotation (marginal note, etc.)	**annotasie**	[annotasi]

footnote	voetnota	[fut·nota]
text	teks	[teks]
type, font	lettertipe	[lɛttər·tipə]
misprint, typo	drukfout	[druk·fæʊt]

translation	vertaling	[fertaliŋ]
to translate (vt)	vertaal	[fertāl]
original (n)	oorspronklike	[oərspronklikə]

famous (adj)	beroemd	[berumt]
unknown (not famous)	onbekend	[onbekent]
interesting (adj)	interessante	[interessantə]
bestseller	blitsverkoper	[blits·ferkopər]

dictionary	woordeboek	[voərdə·buk]
textbook	handboek	[hand·buk]
encyclopedia	ensiklopedie	[ɛŋsiklopedi]

133. Hunting. Fishing

hunting	jag	[jaχ]
to hunt (vi, vt)	jag	[jaχ]
hunter	jagter	[jaχtər]

to shoot (vi)	skiet	[skit]
rifle	geweer	[χeveər]
bullet (shell)	patroon	[patroən]
shot (lead balls)	hael	[haəl]

steel trap	slagyster	[slaχ·ajstər]
snare (for birds, etc.)	valstrik	[falstrik]
to fall into the steel trap	in die valstrik trap	[in di falstrik trap]
to lay a steel trap	n valstrik lê	[ə falstrik lɛ:]

| poacher | wildstroper | [vilt·stropər] |
| game (in hunting) | wild | [vilt] |

hound dog	jaghond	[jaχ·hont]
safari	safari	[safari]
mounted animal	opgestopte dier	[opχestoptə dir]

fisherman, angler	visterman	[fisterman]
fishing (angling)	vis vang	[fis faŋ]
to fish (vi)	vis vang	[fis faŋ]

fishing rod	visstok	[fis·stok]
fishing line	vislyn	[fis·lajn]
hook	vishoek	[fis·huk]
float, bobber	vlotter	[flottər]
bait	aas	[ās]

to cast a line	lyngooi	[lajnχoj]
to bite (ab. fish)	byt	[bajt]
catch (of fish)	vang	[faŋ]
ice-hole	gat in die ys	[χat in di ajs]

fishing net	visnet	[fis·net]
boat	boot	[boət]

to cast[throw] the net	die net gooi	[di net χoj]
to haul the net in	die net intrek	[di net intrek]
to fall into the net	in die net val	[in di net fal]

whaler (person)	walvisvanger	[valfis·vaŋər]
whaleboat	walvisboot	[valfis·boət]
harpoon	harpoen	[harpun]

134. Games. Billiards

billiards	biljart	[biljart]
billiard room, hall	biljartkamer	[biljart·kamər]
ball (snooker, etc.)	bal	[bal]

cue	biljartstok	[biljart·stok]
pocket	sakkie	[sakki]

135. Games. Playing cards

diamonds	diamante	[diamantə]
spades	skoppens	[skoppɛns]
hearts	harte	[hartə]
clubs	klawers	[klavərs]

ace	aas	[ãs]
king	koning	[koniŋ]
queen	dame	[damə]
jack, knave	boer	[bur]

playing card	speelkaart	[speəl·kãrt]
cards	kaarte	[kãrtə]

trump	troefkaart	[truf·kãrt]
deck of cards	pak kaarte	[pak kãrtə]

point	punt	[punt]
to deal (vi, vt)	uitdeel	[œitdeəl]
to shuffle (cards)	skommel	[skomməl]
lead, turn (n)	beurt	[bøərt]
cardsharp	valsspeler	[fals·spelər]

136. Rest. Games. Miscellaneous

to stroll (vi, vt)	**wandel**	[vandəl]
stroll (leisurely walk)	**wandeling**	[vandəliŋ]
car ride	**motorrit**	[motor·rit]
adventure	**avontuur**	[afontɪr]
picnic	**piekniek**	[piknik]
game (chess, etc.)	**spel**	[spel]
player	**speler**	[spelər]
game (one ~ of chess)	**spel**	[spel]
collector (e.g., philatelist)	**versamelaar**	[fersamelãr]
to collect (stamps, etc.)	**versamel**	[fersaməl]
collection	**versameling**	[fersaməliŋ]
crossword puzzle	**blokkiesraaisel**	[blokkis·rãisəl]
racetrack	**perderesiesbaan**	[perdə·resisbãn]
(horse racing venue)		
disco (discotheque)	**disko**	[disko]
sauna	**sauna**	[sɔuna]
lottery	**lotery**	[loteraj]
camping trip	**kampeeruitstappie**	[kampeər·ajtstappi]
camp	**kamp**	[kamp]
tent (for camping)	**tent**	[tɛnt]
compass	**kompas**	[kompas]
camper	**kampeerder**	[kampeərdər]
to watch (movie, etc.)	**kyk**	[kajk]
viewer	**kyker**	[kajkər]
TV show (TV program)	**TV-program**	[te·fe-proχram]

137. Photography

camera (photo)	**kamera**	[kamera]
photo, picture	**foto**	[foto]
photographer	**fotograaf**	[fotoχrãf]
photo studio	**fotostudio**	[foto·studio]
photo album	**fotoalbum**	[foto·album]
camera lens	**kameralens**	[kamera·lɛŋs]
telephoto lens	**telefotolens**	[telefoto·lɛŋs]
filter	**filter**	[filtər]
lens	**lens**	[lɛŋs]
optics (high-quality ~)	**optiek**	[optik]
diaphragm (aperture)	**diafragma**	[diafraχma]

| exposure time (shutter speed) | beligtingstyd | [beliχtiŋs·tajt] |
| viewfinder | soeker | [sukər] |

digital camera	digitale kamera	[diχitalə kamera]
tripod	driepoot	[dripoət]
flash	flits	[flits]

to photograph (vt)	fotografeer	[fotoχrafeər]
to take pictures	fotografeer	[fotoχrafeər]
to have one's picture taken	jou portret laat maak	[jæʊ portret lāt māk]

focus	fokus	[fokus]
to focus	fokus	[fokus]
sharp, in focus (adj)	skerp	[skerp]
sharpness	skerpheid	[skerphæjt]

| contrast | kontras | [kontras] |
| contrast (as adj) | kontrasryk | [kontrasrajk] |

picture (photo)	kiekie	[kiki]
negative (n)	negatief	[neχatif]
film (a roll of ~)	rolfilm	[rolfilm]
frame (still)	raampie	[rāmpi]
to print (photos)	druk	[druk]

138. Beach. Swimming

beach	strand	[strant]
sand	sand	[sant]
deserted (beach)	verlate	[ferlatə]

suntan	sonbruin kleur	[sonbrœin kløər]
to get a tan	bruinbrand	[brœinbrant]
tan (adj)	bruingebrand	[brœiŋəbrant]
sunscreen	sonskermroom	[soŋ·skerm·roəm]

bikini	bikini	[bikini]
bathing suit	baaikostuum	[bāj·kostɪm]
swim trunks	baaibroek	[bāj·bruk]

swimming pool	swembad	[swem·bat]
to swim (vi)	swem	[swem]
shower	stort	[stort]
to change (one's clothes)	verklee	[ferkleə]
towel	handdoek	[handduk]

boat	boot	[boət]
motorboat	motorboot	[motor·boət]
water ski	waterski	[vatər·ski]

paddle boat	**waterfiets**	[vatər·fits]
surfing	**branderplankry**	[brandərplank·raj]
surfer	**branderplankryer**	[brandərplank·rajer]
scuba set	**duiklong**	[dœikloŋ]
flippers (swim fins)	**paddavoet**	[padda·fut]
mask (diving ~)	**duikmasker**	[dœik·maskər]
diver	**duiker**	[dœikər]
to dive (vi)	**duik**	[dœik]
underwater (adv)	**onder water**	[ondər vatər]
beach umbrella	**strandsambreel**	[strand·sambreəl]
sunbed (lounger)	**strandstoel**	[strand·stul]
sunglasses	**sonbril**	[son·bril]
air mattress	**opblaasmatras**	[opblās·matras]
to play (amuse oneself)	**speel**	[speəl]
to go for a swim	**gaan swem**	[χān swem]
beach ball	**strandbal**	[strand·bal]
to inflate (vt)	**opblaas**	[opblās]
inflatable, air (adj)	**opblaas-**	[opblās-]
wave	**golf**	[χolf]
buoy (line of ~s)	**boei**	[bui]
to drown (ab. person)	**verdrink**	[ferdrink]
to save, to rescue	**red**	[ret]
life vest	**reddingsbaadjie**	[rɛddiŋs·bādʒi]
to observe, to watch	**dophou**	[dophæʊ]
lifeguard	**lewensredder**	[levɛŋs·rɛddər]

TECHNICAL EQUIPMENT. TRANSPORTATION

Technical equipment

139. Computer

computer	**rekenaar**	[rekənãr]
notebook, laptop	**skootrekenaar**	[skoet·rekənãr]
to turn on	**aanskakel**	[ãŋskakəl]
to turn off	**afskakel**	[afskakəl]
keyboard	**toetsbord**	[tuts·bort]
key	**toets**	[tuts]
mouse	**muis**	[mœis]
mouse pad	**muismatjie**	[mœis·maki]
button	**knop**	[knop]
cursor	**loper**	[lopər]
monitor	**monitor**	[monitor]
screen	**skerm**	[skerm]
hard disk	**harde skyf**	[hardə skajf]
hard disk capacity	**harde skyf se vermoë**	[hardə skajf sə fermoɛ]
memory	**geheue**	[χəhøə]
random access memory	**RAM-geheue**	[ram-χehøəə]
file	**lêer**	[lɛər]
folder	**gids**	[χids]
to open (vt)	**oopmaak**	[oəpmãk]
to close (vt)	**sluit**	[slœit]
to save (vt)	**bewaar**	[bevãr]
to delete (vt)	**uitvee**	[œitfeə]
to copy (vt)	**kopieer**	[kopir]
to sort (vt)	**sorteer**	[sorteər]
to transfer (copy)	**oorplaas**	[oərplãs]
program	**program**	[proχram]
software	**sagteware**	[saχtevarə]
programmer	**programmeur**	[proχrammøer]
to program (vt)	**programmeer**	[proχrammeər]
hacker	**kuberkraker**	[kubər·krakər]
password	**wagwoord**	[vaχ·woərt]

virus	virus	[firus]
to find, to detect	opspoor	[opspoər]
byte	greep	[χreəp]
megabyte	megagreep	[meχaχreəp]
data	data	[data]
database	databasis	[data·basis]
cable (USB, etc.)	kabel	[kabəl]
to disconnect (vt)	ontkoppel	[ontkoppəl]
to connect (sth to sth)	konnekteer	[konnekteər]

140. Internet. E-mail

Internet	internet	[internet]
browser	webblaaier	[veb·blājer]
search engine	soekenjin	[suk·ɛnʤin]
provider	verskaffer	[ferskaffər]
webmaster	webmeester	[veb·meestər]
website	webwerf	[veb·werf]
webpage	webblad	[veb·blat]
address (e-mail ~)	adres	[adres]
address book	adresboek	[adres·buk]
mailbox	posbus	[pos·bus]
mail	pos	[pos]
full (adj)	vol	[fol]
message	boodskap	[boədskap]
incoming messages	inkomende boodskappe	[inkomendə boədskappə]
outgoing messages	uitgaande boodskappe	[œitχāndə boədskappə]
sender	sender	[sendər]
to send (vt)	verstuur	[ferstɪr]
sending (of mail)	versending	[fersendiŋ]
receiver	ontvanger	[ontfaŋər]
to receive (vt)	ontvang	[ontfaŋ]
correspondence	korrespondensie	[korrespondɛŋsi]
to correspond (vi)	korrespondeer	[korrespondeər]
file	lêer	[lɛər]
to download (vt)	aflaai	[aflāi]
to create (vt)	skep	[skep]
to delete (vt)	uitvee	[œitfeə]
deleted (adj)	uitgevee	[œitχefeə]

connection (ADSL, etc.)	**konneksie**	[konneksi]
speed	**spoed**	[sput]
modem	**modem**	[modem]
access	**toegang**	[tuχaŋ]
port (e.g., input ~)	**portaal**	[portāl]
connection (make a ~)	**aansluiting**	[āŋslœitiŋ]
to connect to ... (vi)	**aansluit by ...**	[āŋslœit baj ...]
to select (vt)	**kies**	[kis]
to search (for ...)	**soek**	[suk]

Transportation

141. Airplane

airplane	**vliegtuig**	[fliχtœiχ]
air ticket	**lugkaartjie**	[luχ·kārki]
airline	**lugredery**	[luχrederaj]
airport	**lughawe**	[luχhavə]
supersonic (adj)	**supersonies**	[supersonis]
captain	**kaptein**	[kaptæjn]
crew	**bemanning**	[bemanniŋ]
pilot	**piloot**	[piloət]
flight attendant (fem.)	**lugwaardin**	[luχ·wārdin]
navigator	**navigator**	[nafiχator]
wings	**vlerke**	[flerkə]
tail	**stert**	[stert]
cockpit	**stuurkajuit**	[stɪr·kajœit]
engine	**enjin**	[ɛnʤin]
undercarriage (landing gear)	**landingstel**	[landiŋ·stəl]
turbine	**turbine**	[turbinə]
propeller	**skroef**	[skruf]
black box	**swart boks**	[swart boks]
yoke (control column)	**stuurstang**	[stɪr·staŋ]
fuel	**brandstof**	[brantstof]
safety card	**veiligheidskaart**	[fæjliχæjts·kārt]
oxygen mask	**suurstofmasker**	[sɪrstof·maskər]
uniform	**uniform**	[uniform]
life vest	**reddingsbaadjie**	[rɛddiŋs·bāʤi]
parachute	**valskerm**	[fal·skerm]
takeoff	**opstyging**	[opstajχiŋ]
to take off (vi)	**opstyg**	[opstajχ]
runway	**landingsbaan**	[landiŋs·bān]
visibility	**uitsig**	[œitsəχ]
flight (act of flying)	**vlug**	[fluχ]
altitude	**hoogte**	[hoəχtə]
air pocket	**lugsak**	[luχsak]
seat	**sitplek**	[sitplek]
headphones	**koptelefoon**	[kop·telefoən]

folding tray (tray table)	voutafeltjie	[fæʊ·tafɛlki]
airplane window	vliegtuigvenster	[fliχtœiχ·fɛŋstər]
aisle	paadjie	[pādʒi]

142. Train

train	trein	[træjn]
commuter train	voorstedelike trein	[foərstedelikə træjn]
express train	sneltrein	[snɛl·træjn]
diesel locomotive	diesellokomotief	[disəl·lokomotif]
steam locomotive	stoomlokomotief	[stoəm·lokomotif]

| passenger car | passasierswa | [passasirs·wa] |
| dining car | eetwa | [eət·wa] |

rails	spoorstawe	[spoər·stawə]
railroad	spoorweg	[spoər·weχ]
railway tie	dwarslëer	[dwarslɛər]

platform (railway ~)	perron	[perron]
track (~ 1, 2, etc.)	spoor	[spoər]
semaphore	semafoor	[semafoər]
station	stasie	[stasi]

engineer (train driver)	treindrywer	[træjn·drajvər]
porter (of luggage)	portier	[portir]
car attendant	kondukteur	[konduktøər]
passenger	passasier	[passasir]
conductor (ticket inspector)	kondukteur	[konduktøər]

| corridor (in train) | gang | [χaŋ] |
| emergency brake | noodrem | [noədrem] |

compartment	kompartiment	[kompartiment]
berth	bed	[bet]
upper berth	boonste bed	[boəŋstə bet]
lower berth	onderste bed	[ondərstə bet]
bed linen, bedding	beddegoed	[beddə·χut]

ticket	kaartjie	[kārki]
schedule	diensrooster	[diŋs·roəstər]
information display	informasiebord	[informasi·bort]

to leave, to depart	vertrek	[fertrek]
departure (of train)	vertrek	[fertrek]
to arrive (ab. train)	aankom	[ānkom]
arrival	aankoms	[ānkoms]
to arrive by train	aankom per trein	[ānkom pər træjn]
to get on the train	in die trein klim	[in di træjn klim]

to get off the train	uit die trein klim	[œit di træjn klim]
train wreck	treinbotsing	[træjn·botsiŋ]
to derail (vi)	ontspoor	[ontspoər]

steam locomotive	stoomlokomotief	[stoəm·lokomotif]
stoker, fireman	stoker	[stokər]
firebox	stookplek	[stoəkplek]
coal	steenkool	[steən·koəl]

143. Ship

| ship | skip | [skip] |
| vessel | vaartuig | [fārtœiχ] |

steamship	stoomboot	[stoəm·boət]
riverboat	rivierboot	[rifir·boət]
cruise ship	toerskip	[tur·skip]
cruiser	kruiser	[krœisər]

yacht	jag	[jaχ]
tugboat	sleepboot	[sleəp·boət]
barge	vragskuit	[fraχ·skœit]
ferry	veerboot	[feər·boət]

| sailing ship | seilskip | [sæjl·skip] |
| brigantine | skoenerbrik | [skunər·brik] |

| ice breaker | ysbreker | [ajs·brekər] |
| submarine | duikboot | [dœik·boət] |

boat (flat-bottomed ~)	roeiboot	[ruiboət]
dinghy	bootjie	[boəki]
lifeboat	reddingsboot	[rɛddiŋs·boət]
motorboat	motorboot	[motor·boət]

captain	kaptein	[kaptæjn]
seaman	seeman	[seəman]
sailor	matroos	[matroəs]
crew	bemanning	[bemanniŋ]

boatswain	bootsman	[boətsman]
ship's boy	skeepsjonge	[skeəps·joŋə]
cook	kok	[kok]
ship's doctor	skeepsdokter	[skeəps·doktər]

deck	dek	[dek]
mast	mas	[mas]
sail	seil	[sæjl]
hold	skeepsruim	[skeəps·rœim]
bow (prow)	boeg	[buχ]

stern	**agterstewe**	[aχtərstevə]
oar	**roeispaan**	[ruis·pān]
screw propeller	**skroef**	[skruf]
cabin	**kajuit**	[kajœit]
wardroom	**offisierskajuit**	[offisirs·kajœit]
engine room	**enjinkamer**	[ɛnʤin·kamər]
bridge	**brug**	[bruχ]
radio room	**radiokamer**	[radio·kamər]
wave (radio)	**golf**	[χolf]
logbook	**logboek**	[loχbuk]
spyglass	**verkyker**	[ferkajkər]
bell	**bel**	[bəl]
flag	**vlag**	[flaχ]
hawser (mooring ~)	**kabel**	[kabəl]
knot (bowline, etc.)	**knoop**	[knoəp]
deckrails	**dekleuning**	[dek·løəniŋ]
gangway	**gangplank**	[χaŋ·plank]
anchor	**anker**	[ankər]
to weigh anchor	**anker lig**	[ankər ləχ]
to drop anchor	**anker uitgooi**	[ankər œitχoj]
anchor chain	**ankerketting**	[ankər·kɛttiŋ]
port (harbor)	**hawe**	[havə]
quay, wharf	**kaai**	[kāi]
to berth (moor)	**vasmeer**	[fasmeər]
to cast off	**vertrek**	[fertrek]
trip, voyage	**reis**	[ræjs]
cruise (sea trip)	**cruise**	[kru:s]
course (route)	**koers**	[kurs]
route (itinerary)	**roete**	[rutə]
fairway (safe water channel)	**vaarwater**	[fār·vatər]
shallows	**sandbank**	[sand·bank]
to run aground	**strand**	[strant]
storm	**storm**	[storm]
signal	**sienjaal**	[sinjāl]
to sink (vi)	**sink**	[sink]
Man overboard!	**Man oorboord!**	[man oərboərd!]
SOS (distress signal)	**SOS**	[sos]
ring buoy	**reddingsboei**	[rɛddiŋs·bui]

144. Airport

airport	**lughawe**	[luχhavə]
airplane	**vliegtuig**	[fliχtœiχ]
airline	**lugredery**	[luχrederaj]
air traffic controller	**lugverkeersleier**	[luχˑferkeərsˑlæjer]
departure	**vertrek**	[fertrek]
arrival	**aankoms**	[ānkoms]
to arrive (by plane)	**aankom**	[ānkom]
departure time	**vertrektyd**	[fertrəkˑtajt]
arrival time	**aankomstyd**	[ānkomsˑtajt]
to be delayed	**vertraag wees**	[fertrāχ veəs]
flight delay	**vlugvertraging**	[fluχˑfertraχiŋ]
information board	**informasiebord**	[informasiˑbort]
information	**informasie**	[informasi]
to announce (vt)	**aankondig**	[ānkondəχ]
flight (e.g., next ~)	**vlug**	[fluχ]
customs	**doeane**	[duanə]
customs officer	**doeanebeampte**	[duanəˑbeamptə]
customs declaration	**doeaneverklaring**	[duanəˑferklariŋ]
to fill out (vt)	**invul**	[inful]
passport control	**paspoortkontrole**	[paspoərtˑkontrolə]
luggage	**bagasie**	[baχasi]
hand luggage	**handbagasie**	[handˑbaχasi]
luggage cart	**bagasiekarretjie**	[baχasiˑkarrəki]
landing	**landing**	[landiŋ]
landing strip	**landingsbaan**	[landiŋsˑbān]
to land (vi)	**land**	[lant]
airstairs	**vliegtuigtrap**	[fliχtœiχˑtrap]
check-in	**na die vertrektoonbank**	[na di fertrəkˑtoənbank]
check-in counter	**vertrektoonbank**	[fertrəkˑtoənbank]
to check-in (vi)	**na die vertrektoonbank gaan**	[na di fertrəkˑtoənbank χān]
boarding pass	**instapkaart**	[instapˑkārt]
departure gate	**vertrekuitgang**	[fertrekˑœitχaŋ]
transit	**transito**	[traŋsito]
to wait (vt)	**wag**	[vaχ]
departure lounge	**vertreksaal**	[fertrəkˑsāl]
to see off	**afsien**	[afsin]
to say goodbye	**afskeid neem**	[afskæjt neəm]

145. Bicycle. Motorcycle

bicycle	**fiets**	[fits]
scooter	**bromponie**	[bromponi]
motorcycle, bike	**motorfiets**	[motorfits]
to go by bicycle	**per fiets ry**	[pər fits raj]
handlebars	**stuurstang**	[stɪr·staŋ]
pedal	**pedaal**	[pedãl]
brakes	**remme**	[remmə]
bicycle seat (saddle)	**fietssaal**	[fits·sãl]
pump	**pomp**	[pomp]
luggage rack	**bagasierak**	[baχasi·rak]
front lamp	**fietslamp**	[fits·lamp]
helmet	**helmet**	[hɛlmet]
wheel	**wiel**	[vil]
fender	**modderskerm**	[moddər·skerm]
rim	**velling**	[fɛlliŋ]
spoke	**speek**	[speək]

Cars

146. Types of cars

automobile, car	motor	[motor]
sports car	sportmotor	[sport·motor]
limousine	limousine	[limæʊsinə]
off-road vehicle	veldvoertuig	[fɛlt·furtœiχ]
convertible (n)	met afslaandak	[met afslāndak]
minibus	bussie	[bussi]
ambulance	ambulans	[ambulaŋs]
snowplow	sneeuploeg	[sniʊ·pluχ]
truck	vragmotor	[fraχ·motor]
tanker truck	tenkwa	[tɛnk·wa]
van (small truck)	bestelwa	[bestəl·wa]
road tractor (trailer truck)	padtrekker	[pad·trɛkkər]
trailer	aanhangwa	[ānhaŋ·wa]
comfortable (adj)	gemaklik	[χemaklik]
used (adj)	gebruik	[χebrœik]

147. Cars. Bodywork

hood	enjinkap	[ɛndʒin·kap]
fender	modderskerm	[moddər·skerm]
roof	dak	[dak]
windshield	voorruit	[foər·rœit]
rear-view mirror	truspieël	[tru·spiɛl]
windshield washer	voorruitsproer	[foər·rœitsprur]
windshield wipers	ruitveërs	[rœit·feɛrs]
side window	syvenster	[saj·fɛŋstər]
window lift (power window)	vensterhyser	[fɛŋstər·hajsər]
antenna	lugdraad	[luχdrāt]
sunroof	sondak	[sondak]
bumper	buffer	[buffər]
trunk	bagasiebak	[baχasi·bak]
roof luggage rack	dakreling	[dak·reliŋ]
door	deur	[døər]

| door handle | handvatsel | [hand·fatsəl] |
| door lock | deurslot | [døər·slot] |

license plate	nommerplaat	[nommər·plãt]
muffler	knaldemper	[knal·dempər]
gas tank	petroltenk	[petrol·tɛnk]
tailpipe	uitlaatpyp	[œitlãt·pajp]

gas, accelerator	gaspedaal	[χas·pedãl]
pedal	pedaal	[pedãl]
gas pedal	gaspedaal	[χas·pedãl]

brake	rem	[rem]
brake pedal	rempedaal	[rem·pedãl]
to brake (use the brake)	remtrap	[remtrap]
parking brake	parkeerrem	[parkeər·rem]

clutch	koppelaar	[koppelãr]
clutch pedal	koppelaarpedaal	[koppelãr·pedãl]
clutch disc	koppelaarskyf	[koppelãr·skajf]
shock absorber	skokbreker	[skok·brekər]

| wheel | wiel | [vil] |
| spare tire | spaarwiel | [spãr·wil] |

| tire | band | [bant] |
| hubcap | wieldop | [wil·dop] |

| driving wheels | dryfwiele | [drajf·wilə] |
| front-wheel drive (as adj) | voorwielaandrywing | [foərwil·ãndrajviŋ] |

| rear-wheel drive (as adj) | agterwielaandrywing | [aχtərwil·ãndrajviŋ] |
| all-wheel drive (as adj) | vierwielaandrywing | [firwil·ãndrajviŋ] |

| gearbox | ratkas | [ratkas] |
| automatic (adj) | outomaties | [æʊtomatis] |

| mechanical (adj) | meganies | [meχanis] |
| gear shift | ratwisselaar | [ratwisselãr] |

| headlight | koplig | [kopləχ] |
| headlights | kopligte | [kopliχtə] |

low beam	dempstraal	[demp·strãl]
high beam	hoofstraal	[hoəf·strãl]
brake light	remlig	[remləχ]

parking lights	parkeerlig	[parkeər·ləχ]
hazard lights	gevaarligte	[χefãr·liχtə]
fog lights	mislampe	[mis·lampə]
turn signal	draaiwyser	[drãj·vajsər]
back-up light	trulig	[truləχ]

148. Cars. Passenger compartment

car inside (interior)	**interieur**	[interiøər]
leather (as adj)	**leer-**	[leər-]
velour (as adj)	**fluweel-**	[fluveəl-]
upholstery	**bekleding**	[beklediŋ]
instrument (gage)	**instrument**	[instrument]
dashboard	**voorpaneel**	[foər·paneəl]
speedometer	**spoedmeter**	[spud·metər]
needle (pointer)	**wyster**	[vajstər]
odometer	**afstandmeter**	[afstant·metər]
indicator (sensor)	**sensor**	[sɛŋsor]
level	**vlak**	[flak]
warning light	**waarskulig**	[vārskuləχ]
steering wheel	**stuurwiel**	[stɪr·wil]
horn	**toeter**	[tutər]
button	**knop**	[knop]
switch	**skakelaar**	[skakəlār]
seat	**sitplek**	[sitplek]
backrest	**rugsteun**	[ruχ·støən]
headrest	**kopstut**	[kopstut]
seat belt	**veiligheidsgordel**	[fæjliχæjts·χordəl]
to fasten the belt	**die gordel vasmaak**	[di χordəl fasmāk]
adjustment (of seats)	**verstelling**	[ferstɛlliŋ]
airbag	**lugsak**	[luχsak]
air-conditioner	**lugversorger**	[luχfersorχər]
radio	**radio**	[radio]
CD player	**CD-speler**	[se·de spelər]
to turn on	**aanskakel**	[āŋskakəl]
antenna	**lugdraad**	[luχdrāt]
glove box	**paneelkassie**	[paneəl·kassi]
ashtray	**asbak**	[asbak]

149. Cars. Engine

engine	**enjin**	[ɛnʤin]
motor	**motor**	[motor]
diesel (as adj)	**diesel**	[disəl]
gasoline (as adj)	**petrol**	[petrol]
engine volume	**enjininhoud**	[ɛnʤin·inhæʊt]
power	**krag**	[kraχ]
horsepower	**perdekrag**	[perdə·kraχ]

piston	suier	[sœier]
cylinder	silinder	[silindər]
valve	klep	[klep]

injector	inspuiting	[inspœitiŋ]
generator (alternator)	generator	[χenerator]
carburetor	vergasser	[ferχassər]
motor oil	motorolie	[motor·oli]

radiator	verkoeler	[ferkulər]
coolant	koelmiddel	[kul·middəl]
cooling fan	waaier	[vãjer]

battery (accumulator)	battery	[battəraj]
starter	aansitter	[ãŋsittər]
ignition	ontsteking	[ontstekiŋ]
spark plug	vonkprop	[fonk·prop]

terminal (of battery)	pool	[poəl]
positive terminal	positiewe pool	[positivə poəl]
negative terminal	negatiewe pool	[neχativə poəl]
fuse	sekering	[sekəriŋ]

air filter	lugfilter	[luχ·filtər]
oil filter	oliefilter	[oli·filtər]
fuel filter	brandstoffilter	[brantstof·filtər]

150. Cars. Crash. Repair

car crash	motorbotsing	[motor·botsiŋ]
traffic accident	verkeersongeluk	[ferkeərs·onχəluk]
to crash (into the wall, etc.)	bots	[bots]

to get smashed up	verongeluk	[feronχəluk]
damage	skade	[skadə]
intact (unscathed)	onbeskadig	[onbeskadəχ]

breakdown	onklaar raak	[onklãr rãk]
to break down (vi)	onklaar raak	[onklãr rãk]
towrope	sleeptou	[sleəp·tæʊ]

puncture	papwiel	[pap·wil]
to be flat	pap wees	[pap veəs]
to pump up	oppomp	[oppomp]
pressure	druk	[druk]
to check (to examine)	nagaan	[naχãn]

repair	herstel	[herstəl]
auto repair shop	garage	[χaraʒə]
spare part	onderdeel	[ondərdeəl]

part	onderdeel	[onderdeel]
bolt (with nut)	bout	[bæʊt]
screw (fastener)	skroef	[skruf]
nut	moer	[mur]
washer	waster	[vaster]
bearing	koeëllaer	[kuɛllaer]

tube	pyp	[pajp]
gasket (head ~)	pakstuk	[pakstuk]
cable, wire	kabel	[kabel]

jack	domkrag	[domkraχ]
wrench	moersleutel	[mur·sløetel]
hammer	hamer	[hamer]
pump	pomp	[pomp]
screwdriver	skroewedraaier	[skruvə·drājer]

| fire extinguisher | brandblusser | [brant·blusser] |
| warning triangle | gevaardriehoek | [χefār·drihuk] |

to stall (vi)	stol	[stol]
stall (n)	stol	[stol]
to be broken	stukkend wees	[stukkent veəs]

to overheat (vi)	oorverhit	[oerferhit]
to be clogged up	verstop raak	[ferstop rāk]
to freeze up (pipes, etc.)	vries	[fris]
to burst (vi, ab. tube)	bars	[bars]

pressure	druk	[druk]
level	vlak	[flak]
slack (~ belt)	slap	[slap]

dent	duik	[dœik]
knocking noise (engine)	klopgeluid	[klop·χəlœit]
crack	kraak	[krāk]
scratch	skraap	[skrāp]

151. Cars. Road

road	pad	[pat]
highway	deurpad	[døerpat]
freeway	deurpad	[døerpat]
direction (way)	rigting	[riχtin]
distance	afstand	[afstant]

bridge	brug	[bruχ]
parking lot	parkeerterrein	[parkeer·terræjn]
square	plein	[plæjn]
interchange	padknoop	[pad·knoəp]

tunnel	**tonnel**	[tonnəl]
gas station	**petrolstasie**	[petrol·stasi]
parking lot	**parkeerterrein**	[parkeər·terræjn]
gas pump (fuel dispenser)	**petrolpomp**	[petrol·pomp]
auto repair shop	**garage**	[χaraʒə]
to get gas (to fill up)	**volmaak**	[folmăk]
fuel	**brandstof**	[brantstof]
jerrycan	**petrolblik**	[petrol·blik]
asphalt	**teer**	[teər]
road markings	**padmerktekens**	[pad·merktekɛŋs]
curb	**randsteen**	[rand·steən]
guardrail	**skutreling**	[skut·reliŋ]
ditch	**donga**	[donχa]
roadside (shoulder)	**skouer**	[skæʋər]
lamppost	**lamppaal**	[lamp·păl]
to drive (a car)	**bestuur**	[bestɪr]
to turn (e.g., ~ left)	**draai**	[drăi]
to make a U-turn	**U-draai maak**	[u-drăj măk]
reverse (~ gear)	**tru-**	[tru-]
to honk (vi)	**toeter**	[tutər]
honk (sound)	**toeter**	[tutər]
to get stuck (in the mud, etc.)	**vassteek**	[fassteək]
to spin the wheels	**die wiele laat tol**	[di vilə lăt tol]
to cut, to turn off (vt)	**afskakel**	[afskakəl]
speed	**spoed**	[sput]
to exceed the speed limit	**die spoedgrens oortree**	[di sputχrɛŋs oərtreə]
traffic lights	**robot**	[robot]
driver's license	**bestuurslisensie**	[bestɪrs·lisɛŋsi]
grade crossing	**treinoorgang**	[træjn·oərχaŋ]
intersection	**kruispunt**	[krœis·punt]
crosswalk	**sebraoorgang**	[sebra·oərχaŋ]
bend, curve	**draai**	[drăi]
pedestrian zone	**voetgangerstraat**	[futχaŋər·străt]

PEOPLE. LIFE EVENTS

Life events

152. Holidays. Event

celebration, holiday	**partytjie**	[partajki]
national day	**nasionale dag**	[naʃionalə daχ]
public holiday	**openbare vakansiedag**	[openbarə fakaŋsi·daχ]
to commemorate (vt)	**herdenk**	[herdenk]
event (happening)	**gebeurtenis**	[χebøərtenis]
event (organized activity)	**gebeurtenis**	[χebøərtenis]
banquet (party)	**banket**	[banket]
reception (formal party)	**onthaal**	[onthãl]
feast	**feesmaal**	[fees·mãl]
anniversary	**verjaardag**	[ferjãr·daχ]
jubilee	**jubileum**	[jubiløəm]
to celebrate (vt)	**vier**	[fir]
New Year	**Nuwejaar**	[nuvejãr]
Happy New Year!	**Voorspoedige Nuwejaar**	[foərspudiχə nuvejãr]
Santa Claus	**Kersvader**	[kers·fadər]
Christmas	**Kersfees**	[kersfees]
Merry Christmas!	**Geseënde Kersfees**	[χesɛɛndə kersfeɛs]
Christmas tree	**Kersboom**	[kers·boəm]
fireworks (fireworks show)	**vuurwerk**	[fɪrwerk]
wedding	**bruilof**	[brœilof]
groom	**bruidegom**	[brœidəχom]
bride	**bruid**	[brœit]
to invite (vt)	**uitnooi**	[œitnoj]
invitation card	**uitnodiging**	[œitnodəχin]
guest	**gas**	[χas]
to visit	**besoek**	[besuk]
(~ your parents, etc.)		
to meet the guests	**die gaste ontmoet**	[di χastə ontmut]
gift, present	**present**	[present]
to give (sth as present)	**gee**	[χeə]
to receive gifts	**presente ontvang**	[presentə ontfaŋ]

bouquet (of flowers)	**boeket**	[buket]
congratulations	**gelukwense**	[χelukwɛŋsə]
to congratulate (vt)	**gelukwens**	[χelukwɛŋs]
greeting card	**geleentheidskaartjie**	[χeleenthæjts·kãrki]
toast	**heildronk**	[hæjldronk]
to offer (a drink, etc.)	**aanbied**	[ãnbit]
champagne	**sjampanje**	[ʃampanje]
to enjoy oneself	**jouself geniet**	[jæusɛlf χenit]
merriment (gaiety)	**pret**	[pret]
joy (emotion)	**vreugde**	[frøəχdə]
dance	**dans**	[daŋs]
to dance (vi, vt)	**dans**	[daŋs]
waltz	**wals**	[vals]
tango	**tango**	[tanχo]

153. Funerals. Burial

cemetery	**begraafplaas**	[beχrãf·plãs]
grave, tomb	**graf**	[χraf]
cross	**kruis**	[krœis]
gravestone	**grafsteen**	[χrafsteən]
fence	**heining**	[hæjniŋ]
chapel	**kapel**	[kapəl]
death	**dood**	[doət]
to die (vi)	**doodgaan**	[doədχãn]
the deceased	**oorledene**	[oərledenə]
mourning	**rou**	[ræʊ]
to bury (vt)	**begrawe**	[beχravə]
funeral home	**begrafnisonderneming**	[beχrafnis·ondərnemiŋ]
funeral	**begrafnis**	[beχrafnis]
wreath	**krans**	[kraŋs]
casket, coffin	**doodskis**	[doədskis]
hearse	**lykswa**	[lajks·wa]
shroud	**lykkleed**	[lajk·kleət]
funeral procession	**begrafnisstoet**	[beχrafnis·stut]
funerary urn	**urn**	[urn]
crematory	**krematorium**	[krematorium]
obituary	**doodsberig**	[doəds·berəχ]
to cry (weep)	**huil**	[hœil]
to sob (vi)	**snik**	[snik]

154. War. Soldiers

platoon	**peleton**	[peleton]
company	**kompanie**	[kompani]
regiment	**regiment**	[reχiment]
army	**leër**	[leɛr]
division	**divisie**	[difisi]
section, squad	**afdeling**	[afdeliŋ]
host (army)	**leërskare**	[leɛrskarə]
soldier	**soldaat**	[soldãt]
officer	**offisier**	[offisir]
private	**soldaat**	[soldãt]
sergeant	**sersant**	[sersant]
lieutenant	**luitenant**	[lœitənant]
captain	**kaptein**	[kaptæjn]
major	**majoor**	[majoər]
colonel	**kolonel**	[kolonəl]
general	**generaal**	[χenerãl]
sailor	**matroos**	[matroəs]
captain	**kaptein**	[kaptæjn]
boatswain	**bootsman**	[boətsman]
artilleryman	**artilleris**	[artilleris]
paratrooper	**valskermsoldaat**	[falskerm·soldãt]
pilot	**piloot**	[piloət]
navigator	**navigator**	[nafiχator]
mechanic	**werktuigkundige**	[verktœiχ·kundiχə]
pioneer (sapper)	**sappeur**	[sappøər]
parachutist	**valskermspringer**	[falskerm·spriŋər]
reconnaissance scout	**verkenner**	[ferkɛnnər]
sniper	**skerpskut**	[skerp·skut]
patrol (group)	**patrollie**	[patrolli]
to patrol (vt)	**patrolleer**	[patrolleər]
sentry, guard	**wag**	[vaχ]
warrior	**vegter**	[feχtər]
patriot	**patriot**	[patriot]
hero	**held**	[hɛlt]
heroine	**heldin**	[hɛldin]
traitor	**verraaier**	[ferrãjer]
to betray (vt)	**verraai**	[ferrãi]
deserter	**droster**	[drostər]
to desert (vi)	**dros**	[dros]

mercenary	huursoldaat	[hɪr·soldāt]
recruit	rekruteer	[rekruteər]
volunteer	vrywilliger	[frajvillixər]

dead (n)	dooie	[doje]
wounded (n)	gewonde	[xevondə]
prisoner of war	krygsgevangene	[krajxs·xefaŋənə]

155. War. Military actions. Part 1

war	oorlog	[oərloχ]
to be at war	oorlog voer	[oərloχ fur]
civil war	burgeroorlog	[burgər·oərloχ]

treacherously (adv)	valslik	[falslik]
declaration of war	oorlogsverklaring	[oərloχs·ferklariŋ]
to declare (~ war)	oorlog verklaar	[oərloχ fərklār]
aggression	aggressie	[aχrɛssi]
to attack (invade)	aanval	[ānfal]

to invade (vt)	binneval	[binnəfal]
invader	binnevaller	[binnəfallər]
conqueror	veroweraar	[feroverār]

defense	verdediging	[ferdedəχiŋ]
to defend (a country, etc.)	verdedig	[ferdedəχ]
to defend (against ...)	jouself verdedig	[jæʊsɛlf ferdedəχ]

enemy	vyand	[fajant]
foe, adversary	teëstander	[teɛstandər]
enemy (as adj)	vyandig	[fajandəχ]

| strategy | strategie | [strateχi] |
| tactics | taktiek | [taktik] |

order	bevel	[befəl]
command (order)	bevel	[befəl]
to order (vt)	beveel	[befeəl]
mission	opdrag	[opdraχ]
secret (adj)	geheim	[χəhæejm]

| battle | veldslag | [fɛltslaχ] |
| combat | geveg | [χefeχ] |

attack	aanval	[ānfal]
charge (assault)	bestorming	[bestormiŋ]
to storm (vt)	bestorm	[bestorm]
siege (to be under ~)	beleg	[beleχ]
offensive (n)	aanval	[ānfal]
to go on the offensive	tot die offensief oorgaan	[tot di offɛnsif oərχān]

retreat	terugtrekking	[teruχ·trɛkkiŋ]
to retreat (vi)	terugtrek	[teruχtrek]
encirclement	omsingeling	[omsinχəliŋ]
to encircle (vt)	omsingel	[omsiŋəl]
bombing (by aircraft)	bombardement	[bombardɛment]
to bomb (vt)	bombardeer	[bombardeər]
explosion	ontploffing	[ontploffiŋ]
shot	skoot	[skoət]
firing (burst of ~)	skiet	[skit]
to aim (to point a weapon)	mik op	[mik op]
to point (a gun)	rig	[riχ]
to hit (the target)	tref	[tref]
to sink (~ a ship)	sink	[sink]
hole (in a ship)	gat	[χat]
to founder, to sink (vi)	sink	[sink]
front (war ~)	front	[front]
evacuation	evakuasie	[ɛfakuasi]
to evacuate (vt)	evakueer	[ɛfakueər]
trench	loopgraaf	[loəpχrāf]
barbwire	doringdraad	[doriŋ·drāt]
barrier (anti tank ~)	versperring	[fersperriŋ]
watchtower	wagtoring	[vaχ·toriŋ]
military hospital	militêre hospitaal	[militærə hospitāl]
to wound (vt)	wond	[vont]
wound	wond	[vont]
wounded (n)	gewonde	[χevondə]
to be wounded	gewond	[χevont]
serious (wound)	ernstig	[ɛrnstəχ]

156. Weapons

weapons	wapens	[vapɛns]
firearms	vuurwapens	[fɪr·vapɛns]
cold weapons (knives, etc.)	messe	[mɛssə]
chemical weapons	chemiese wapens	[χemisə vapɛns]
nuclear (adj)	kern-	[kern-]
nuclear weapons	kernwapens	[kern·vapɛns]
bomb	bom	[bom]
atomic bomb	atoombom	[atoəm·bom]

pistol (gun)	**pistool**	[pistoəl]
rifle	**geweer**	[χeveər]
submachine gun	**aanvalsgeweer**	[ānvals·χeveər]
machine gun	**masjiengeweer**	[maʃin·χeveər]
muzzle	**loop**	[loəp]
barrel	**loop**	[loəp]
caliber	**kaliber**	[kalibər]
trigger	**sneller**	[snɛllər]
sight (aiming device)	**visier**	[fisir]
magazine	**magasyn**	[maχasajn]
butt (shoulder stock)	**kolf**	[kolf]
hand grenade	**handgranaat**	[hand·χranāt]
explosive	**springstof**	[spriŋstof]
bullet	**koeël**	[kuɛl]
cartridge	**patroon**	[patroən]
charge	**lading**	[ladiŋ]
ammunition	**ammunisie**	[ammunisi]
bomber (aircraft)	**bomwerper**	[bom·werpər]
fighter	**straalvegter**	[strāl·feχtər]
helicopter	**helikopter**	[helikoptər]
anti-aircraft gun	**lugafweer**	[luχafweər]
tank	**tenk**	[tɛnk]
tank gun	**tenkkanon**	[tɛnk·kanon]
artillery	**artillerie**	[artilleri]
gun (cannon, howitzer)	**kanon**	[kanon]
to lay (a gun)	**aanlê**	[ānlɛ:]
shell (projectile)	**projektiel**	[projektil]
mortar bomb	**mortierbom**	[mortir·bom]
mortar	**mortier**	[mortir]
splinter (shell fragment)	**skrapnel**	[skrapnəl]
submarine	**duikboot**	[dœik·boət]
torpedo	**torpedo**	[torpedo]
missile	**vuurpyl**	[fɪr·pajl]
to load (gun)	**laai**	[lāi]
to shoot (vi)	**skiet**	[skit]
to point at (the cannon)	**rig op**	[riχ op]
bayonet	**bajonet**	[bajonet]
rapier	**rapier**	[rapir]
saber (e.g., cavalry ~)	**sabel**	[sabəl]
spear (weapon)	**spies**	[spis]
bow	**boog**	[boəχ]

arrow	**pyl**	[pajl]
musket	**musket**	[musket]
crossbow	**kruisboog**	[krœis·boeχ]

157. Ancient people

primitive (prehistoric)	**primitief**	[primitif]
prehistoric (adj)	**prehistories**	[prehistoris]
ancient (~ civilization)	**antiek**	[antik]

Stone Age	**Steentydperk**	[steen·tajtperk]
Bronze Age	**Bronstydperk**	[brɔŋs·tajtperk]
Ice Age	**Ystydperk**	[ajs·tajtperk]

tribe	**stam**	[stam]
cannibal	**mensvreter**	[mɛŋs·fretər]
hunter	**jagter**	[jaχtər]
to hunt (vi, vt)	**jag**	[jaχ]
mammoth	**mammoet**	[mammut]

cave	**grot**	[χrot]
fire	**vuur**	[fɪr]
campfire	**kampvuur**	[kampfɪr]
cave painting	**rotstekening**	[rots·tekəniŋ]

tool (e.g., stone ax)	**werktuig**	[verktœiχ]
spear	**spies**	[spis]
stone ax	**klipbyl**	[klip·bajl]
to be at war	**oorlog voer**	[oərloχ fur]
to domesticate (vt)	**tem**	[tem]

idol	**afgod**	[afχot]
to worship (vt)	**aanbid**	[ānbit]
superstition	**bygeloof**	[bajχəloəf]
rite	**ritueel**	[ritueəl]

| evolution | **evolusie** | [ɛfolusi] |
| development | **ontwikkeling** | [ontwikkeliŋ] |

| disappearance (extinction) | **verdwyning** | [ferdwajniŋ] |
| to adapt oneself | **jou aanpas** | [jæʊ ānpas] |

archeology	**argeologie**	[arχeoloχi]
archeologist	**argeoloog**	[arχeoloəχ]
archeological (adj)	**argeologies**	[arχeoloχis]

excavation site	**opgrawingsplek**	[opχraviŋs·plek]
excavations	**opgrawingsplekke**	[opχraviŋs·plɛkkə]
find (object)	**vonds**	[fonds]
fragment	**fragment**	[fraχment]

158. Middle Ages

people (ethnic group)	volk	[folk]
peoples	bevolking	[befolkiŋ]
tribe	stam	[stam]
tribes	stamme	[stammə]

barbarians	barbare	[barbarə]
Gauls	Galliërs	[χalliɛrs]
Goths	Gote	[χote]
Slavs	Slawe	[slavə]
Vikings	Vikings	[vikiŋs]

Romans	Romeine	[romæjnə]
Roman (adj)	Romeins	[romæjns]

Byzantines	Bisantyne	[bisantajnə]
Byzantium	Bisantium	[bisantium]
Byzantine (adj)	Bisantyns	[bisantajns]

emperor	keiser	[kæjsər]
leader, chief (tribal ~)	leier	[læjer]
powerful (~ king)	magtig	[maχtəχ]
king	koning	[koniŋ]
ruler (sovereign)	heerser	[heərsər]

knight	ridder	[riddər]
feudal lord	feodale heerser	[feodalə heərsər]
feudal (adj)	feodaal	[feodãl]
vassal	vasal	[fasal]

duke	hertog	[hertoχ]
earl	graaf	[χrãf]
baron	baron	[baron]
bishop	biskop	[biskop]

armor	harnas	[harnas]
shield	skild	[skilt]
sword	swaard	[swãrt]
visor	visier	[fisir]
chainmail	maliehemp	[mali·hemp]

Crusade	Kruistog	[krœis·toχ]
crusader	kruisvaarder	[krœis·fãrdər]

territory	gebied	[χebit]
to attack (invade)	aanval	[ãnfal]
to conquer (vt)	verower	[ferovər]
to occupy (invade)	beset	[beset]
siege (to be under ~)	beleg	[beleχ]
besieged (adj)	beleërde	[beleɛrdə]

to besiege (vt)	beleër	[beleɛr]
inquisition	inkwisisie	[inkvisisi]
inquisitor	inkwisiteur	[inkvisitøər]
torture	marteling	[martəliŋ]
cruel (adj)	wreed	[vreət]
heretic	ketter	[kɛttər]
heresy	kettery	[kɛtteraj]

seafaring	seevaart	[seə·fãrt]
pirate	piraat, seerower	[pirãt], [seə·rovər]
piracy	piratery, seerowery	[pirateraj], [seə·roveraj]
boarding (attack)	enter	[ɛntər]
loot, booty	buit	[bœit]
treasures	skatte	[skattə]

discovery	ontdekking	[ontdɛkkiŋ]
to discover (new land, etc.)	ontdek	[ontdek]
expedition	ekspedisie	[ɛkspedisi]

musketeer	musketier	[musketir]
cardinal	kardinaal	[kardinãl]
heraldry	heraldiek	[heraldik]
heraldic (adj)	heraldies	[heraldis]

159. Leader. Chief. Authorities

king	koning	[koniŋ]
queen	koningin	[koniŋin]
royal (adj)	koninklik	[koninklik]
kingdom	koninkryk	[koninkrajk]

prince	prins	[prins]
princess	prinses	[prinsəs]

president	president	[president]
vice-president	vise-president	[fise-president]
senator	senator	[senator]

monarch	monarg	[monarχ]
ruler (sovereign)	heerser	[heərsər]
dictator	diktator	[diktator]
tyrant	tiran	[tiran]
magnate	magnaat	[maχnãt]

director	direkteur	[direktøər]
chief	baas	[bãs]
manager (director)	bestuurder	[bestɪrdər]
boss	baas	[bãs]
owner	eienaar	[æjenãr]
leader	leier	[læjer]

head (~ of delegation)	hoof	[hoəf]
authorities	outoriteite	[æʊtoritæjtə]
superiors	hoofde	[hoəfdə]

governor	goewerneur	[χuvernøər]
consul	konsul	[koŋsul]
diplomat	diplomaat	[diplomãt]
mayor	burgermeester	[burgər·meəstər]
sheriff	sheriff	[sheriff]

emperor	keiser	[kæjsər]
tsar, czar	tsaar	[tsãr]
pharaoh	farao	[farao]
khan	kan	[kan]

160. Breaking the law. Criminals. Part 1

bandit	bandiet	[bandit]
crime	misdaad	[misdãt]
criminal (person)	misdadiger	[misdadiχər]

thief	dief	[dif]
to steal (vi, vt)	steel	[steəl]
stealing (larceny)	steel	[steəl]
theft	diefstal	[difstal]

to kidnap (vt)	ontvoer	[ontfur]
kidnapping	ontvoering	[ontfuriŋ]
kidnapper	ontvoerder	[ontfurdər]

ransom	losgeld	[losχɛlt]
to demand ransom	losgeld eis	[losχɛlt æjs]

to rob (vt)	besteel	[besteəl]
robbery	oorval	[oərfal]
robber	boef	[buf]

to extort (vt)	afpers	[afpers]
extortionist	afperser	[afpersər]
extortion	afpersing	[afpersiŋ]

to murder, to kill	vermoor	[fermoər]
murder	moord	[moərt]
murderer	moordenaar	[moərdenãr]

gunshot	skoot	[skoət]
to shoot to death	doodskiet	[doədskit]
to shoot (vi)	skiet	[skit]
shooting	skietery	[skiteraj]
incident (fight, etc.)	insident	[insident]

fight, brawl	geveg	[ˣefeˣ]
Help!	Help!	[hɛlp!]
victim	slagoffer	[slaˣoffər]

to damage (vt)	beskadig	[beskadəˣ]
damage	skade	[skadə]
dead body, corpse	lyk	[lajk]
grave (~ crime)	ernstig	[ɛrnstəˣ]

to attack (vt)	aanval	[ānfal]
to beat (to hit)	slaan	[slān]
to beat up	platslaan	[platslān]
to take (rob of sth)	vat	[fat]
to stab to death	doodsteek	[doədsteək]
to maim (vt)	vermink	[fermink]
to wound (vt)	wond	[vont]

blackmail	afpersing	[afpersiŋ]
to blackmail (vt)	afpers	[afpers]
blackmailer	afperser	[afpersər]

protection racket	beskermingswendelary	[beskermiŋ·swendəlaraj]
racketeer	afperser	[afpersər]
gangster	boef	[buf]
mafia, Mob	mafia	[mafia]

pickpocket	sakkeroller	[sakkerollər]
burglar	inbreker	[inbrekər]
smuggling	smokkel	[smokkəl]
smuggler	smokkelaar	[smokkəlār]

forgery	vervalsing	[ferfalsiŋ]
to forge (counterfeit)	verval	[ferfal]
fake (forged)	vals	[fals]

161. Breaking the law. Criminals. Part 2

rape	verkragting	[ferkraˣtiŋ]
to rape (vt)	verkrag	[ferkraˣ]
rapist	verkragter	[ferkraˣtər]
maniac	maniak	[maniak]

prostitute (fem.)	prostituut	[prostitɪt]
prostitution	prostitusie	[prostitusi]
pimp	pooier	[pojer]

drug addict	dwelmslaaf	[dwɛlm·slāf]
drug dealer	dwelmhandelaar	[dwɛlm·handəlār]
to blow up (bomb)	opblaas	[opblās]
explosion	ontploffing	[ontploffiŋ]

| to set fire | aan die brand steek | [ān di brant steek] |
| arsonist | brandstigter | [brant·stiχtər] |

terrorism	terrorisme	[terrorismə]
terrorist	terroris	[terroris]
hostage	gyselaar	[χajsəlār]

to swindle (deceive)	bedrieg	[bedrəχ]
swindle, deception	bedrog	[bedroχ]
swindler	bedrieër	[bedriɛr]

to bribe (vt)	omkoop	[omkoəp]
bribery	omkopery	[omkoperaj]
bribe	omkoopgeld	[omkoəp·χɛlt]

poison	gif	[χif]
to poison (vt)	vergiftig	[ferχiftəχ]
to poison oneself	jouself vergiftig	[jæʊsɛlf ferχiftəχ]

| suicide (act) | selfmoord | [sɛlfmoərt] |
| suicide (person) | selfmoordenaar | [sɛlfmoərdenār] |

to threaten (vt)	dreig	[dræjχ]
threat	dreigement	[dræjχement]
attempt (attack)	aanslag	[āŋslaχ]

| to steal (a car) | steel | [steəl] |
| to hijack (a plane) | kaap | [kāp] |

| revenge | wraak | [vrāk] |
| to avenge (get revenge) | wreek | [vreək] |

to torture (vt)	martel	[martəl]
torture	marteling	[martəliŋ]
to torment (vt)	folter	[foltər]

pirate	piraat, seerower	[pirāt], [seə·rovər]
hooligan	skollie	[skolli]
armed (adj)	gewapen	[χevapen]
violence	geweld	[χevɛlt]
illegal (unlawful)	onwettig	[onwɛttəχ]

| spying (espionage) | spioenasie | [spiunasi] |
| to spy (vi) | spioeneer | [spiuneər] |

162. Police. Law. Part 1

justice	justisie	[jəstisi]
court (see you in ~)	geregshof	[χereχshof]
judge	regter	[reχtər]

jurors	jurielede	[jurilede]
jury trial	jurieregspraak	[juri·reχsprāk]
to judge (vt)	bereg	[bereχ]
lawyer, attorney	advokaat	[adfokāt]
defendant	beklaagde	[beklāχde]
dock	beklaagdebank	[beklāχde·bank]
charge	aanklag	[ānklaχ]
accused	beskuldigde	[beskuldiχde]
sentence	vonnis	[fonnis]
to sentence (vt)	veroordeel	[feroerdeel]
guilty (culprit)	skuldig	[skuldeχ]
to punish (vt)	straf	[straf]
punishment	straf	[straf]
fine (penalty)	boete	[bute]
life imprisonment	lewenslange gevangenisstraf	[levɛŋslaŋe χefaŋenis·straf]
death penalty	doodstraf	[doedstraf]
electric chair	elektriese stoel	[ɛlektrise stul]
gallows	galg	[χalχ]
to execute (vt)	eksekuteer	[ɛksekuteer]
execution	eksekusie	[ɛksekusi]
prison, jail	tronk	[tronk]
cell	sel	[sel]
escort	eskort	[ɛskort]
prison guard	tronkbewaarder	[tronk·bevārder]
prisoner	gevangene	[χefaŋene]
handcuffs	handboeie	[hant·buje]
to handcuff (vt)	in die boeie slaan	[in di buje slān]
prison break	ontsnapping	[ontsnappiŋ]
to break out (vi)	ontsnap	[ontsnap]
to disappear (vi)	verdwyn	[ferdwajn]
to release (from prison)	vrylaat	[frajlāt]
amnesty	amnestie	[amnesti]
police	polisie	[polisi]
police officer	polisieman	[polisi·man]
police station	polisiestasie	[polisi·stasi]
billy club	knuppel	[knuppel]
bullhorn	megafoon	[meχafoen]
patrol car	patrolliemotor	[patrolli·motor]
siren	sirene	[sirene]

to turn on the siren	die sirene aanskakel	[di sirenə ãŋskakəl]
siren call	sirenegeloei	[sirenə·χelui]
crime scene	misdaadtoneel	[misdād·toneəl]
witness	getuie	[χetœiə]
freedom	vryheid	[frajhæjt]
accomplice	medepligtige	[medə·pliχtiχə]
to flee (vi)	ontvlug	[ontfluχ]
trace (to leave a ~)	spoor	[spoər]

163. Police. Law. Part 2

search (investigation)	soektog	[suktoχ]
to look for ...	soek ...	[suk ...]
suspicion	verdenking	[ferdɛnkiŋ]
suspicious (e.g., ~ vehicle)	verdag	[ferdaχ]
to stop (cause to halt)	teëhou	[teɛhæʋ]
to detain (keep in custody)	aanhou	[ãnhæʋ]
case (lawsuit)	hofsaak	[hofsāk]
investigation	ondersoek	[ondərsuk]
detective	speurder	[spøərdər]
investigator	speurder	[spøərdər]
hypothesis	hipotese	[hipotesə]
motive	motief	[motif]
interrogation	ondervraging	[ondərfraχiŋ]
to interrogate (vt)	ondervra	[ondərfra]
to question (~ neighbors, etc.)	verhoor	[ferhoər]
check (identity ~)	kontroleer	[kontroleər]
round-up	klopjag	[klopjaχ]
search (~ warrant)	huissoeking	[hœis·sukiŋ]
chase (pursuit)	agtervolging	[aχtərfolχiŋ]
to pursue, to chase	agtervolg	[aχtərfolχ]
to track (a criminal)	opspoor	[opspoər]
arrest	inhegtenisneming	[inheχtenis·nemiŋ]
to arrest (sb)	arresteer	[arresteər]
to catch (thief, etc.)	vang	[faŋ]
capture	opsporing	[opsporiŋ]
document	dokument	[dokument]
proof (evidence)	bewys	[bevajs]
to prove (vt)	bewys	[bevajs]
footprint	voetspoor	[futspoər]
fingerprints	vingerafdrukke	[fiŋər·afdrukkə]
piece of evidence	bewysstuk	[bevajs·stuk]
alibi	alibi	[alibi]

innocent (not guilty)	**onskuldig**	[ɔŋskuldəχ]
injustice	**onreg**	[onreχ]
unjust, unfair (adj)	**onregverdig**	[onreχferdəχ]
criminal (adj)	**krimineel**	[krimineəl]
to confiscate (vt)	**in beslag neem**	[in beslaχ neəm]
drug (illegal substance)	**dwelm**	[dwɛlm]
weapon, gun	**wapen**	[vapen]
to disarm (vt)	**ontwapen**	[ontvapen]
to order (command)	**beveel**	[befeəl]
to disappear (vi)	**verdwyn**	[ferdwajn]
law	**wet**	[vet]
legal, lawful (adj)	**wettig**	[vɛttəχ]
illegal, illicit (adj)	**onwettig**	[onwɛttəχ]
responsibility (blame)	**verantwoordelikheid**	[ferant·voərdelikhæjt]
responsible (adj)	**verantwoordelik**	[ferant·voərdelik]

NATURE

The Earth. Part 1

164. Outer space

space	kosmos	[kosmos]
space (as adj)	kosmies	[kosmis]
outer space	buitenste ruimte	[bœitɛŋstə rajmtə]
world	wêreld	[væːrɛlt]
universe	heelal	[heəlal]
galaxy	sterrestelsel	[sterrə·stɛlsəl]
star	ster	[ster]
constellation	sterrebeeld	[sterrə·beəlt]
planet	planeet	[planeət]
satellite	satelliet	[satɛllit]
meteorite	meteoriet	[meteorit]
comet	komeet	[komeət]
asteroid	asteroïed	[asteroïət]
orbit	baan	[bān]
to revolve (~ around the Earth)	draai	[drāi]
atmosphere	atmosfeer	[atmosfeər]
the Sun	die Son	[di son]
solar system	sonnestelsel	[sonnə·stɛlsəl]
solar eclipse	sonsverduistering	[sɔŋs·ferdœisteriŋ]
the Earth	die Aarde	[di ārdə]
the Moon	die Maan	[di mān]
Mars	Mars	[mars]
Venus	Venus	[fenus]
Jupiter	Jupiter	[jupitər]
Saturn	Saturnus	[saturnus]
Mercury	Mercurius	[merkurius]
Uranus	Uranus	[uranus]
Neptune	Neptunus	[neptunus]
Pluto	Pluto	[pluto]
Milky Way	Melkweg	[melk·weχ]

| Great Bear (Ursa Major) | Groot Beer | [χroət beər] |
| North Star | Poolster | [poəl·stər] |

Martian	marsbewoner	[mars·bevonər]
extraterrestrial (n)	buiteaardse wese	[bœitə·ārdsə vesə]
alien	ruimtewese	[rœimtə·vesə]
flying saucer	vlieënde skottel	[fliɛndə skottəl]

spaceship	ruimteskip	[rœimtə·skip]
space station	ruimtestasie	[rœimtə·stasi]
blast-off	vertrek	[fertrek]

engine	enjin	[ɛnʤin]
nozzle	uitlaatpyp	[œitlāt·pajp]
fuel	brandstof	[brantstof]

cockpit, flight deck	stuurkajuit	[stɪr·kajœit]
antenna	lugdraad	[luχdrāt]
porthole	patryspoort	[patrajs·poərt]
solar panel	sonpaneel	[son·paneəl]
spacesuit	ruimtepak	[rœimtə·pak]

| weightlessness | gewigloosheid | [χeviχloəshæjt] |
| oxygen | suurstof | [sɪrstof] |

| docking (in space) | koppeling | [koppeliŋ] |
| to dock (vi, vt) | koppel | [koppəl] |

observatory	observatorium	[observatorium]
telescope	teleskoop	[teleskoəp]
to observe (vt)	waarneem	[vārneəm]
to explore (vt)	eksploreer	[ɛksploreər]

165. The Earth

the Earth	die Aarde	[di ārdə]
the globe (the Earth)	die aardbol	[di ārdbol]
planet	planeet	[planeət]

atmosphere	atmosfeer	[atmosfeər]
geography	geografie	[χeoχrafi]
nature	natuur	[natɪr]

globe (table ~)	aardbol	[ārd·bol]
map	kaart	[kārt]
atlas	atlas	[atlas]

Europe	Europa	[øəropa]
Asia	Asië	[asiɛ]
Africa	Afrika	[afrika]

Australia	**Australië**	[ɔustraliɛ]
America	**Amerika**	[amerika]
North America	**Noord-Amerika**	[noərd-amerika]
South America	**Suid-Amerika**	[sœid-amerika]
Antarctica	**Suidpool**	[sœid·poəl]
the Arctic	**Noordpool**	[noərd·poəl]

166. Cardinal directions

north	**noorde**	[noərdə]
to the north	**na die noorde**	[na di noərdə]
in the north	**in die noorde**	[in di noərdə]
northern (adj)	**noordelik**	[noərdəlik]
south	**suide**	[sœidə]
to the south	**na die suide**	[na di sœidə]
in the south	**in die suide**	[in di sœidə]
southern (adj)	**suidelik**	[sœidəlik]
west	**weste**	[vestə]
to the west	**na die weste**	[na di vestə]
in the west	**in die weste**	[in di vestə]
western (adj)	**westelik**	[vestelik]
east	**ooste**	[oəstə]
to the east	**na die ooste**	[na di oəstə]
in the east	**in die ooste**	[in di oəstə]
eastern (adj)	**oostelik**	[oəstəlik]

167. Sea. Ocean

sea	**see**	[seə]
ocean	**oseaan**	[oseãn]
gulf (bay)	**golf**	[χolf]
straits	**straat**	[strãt]
land (solid ground)	**land**	[lant]
continent (mainland)	**kontinent**	[kontinent]
island	**eiland**	[æjlant]
peninsula	**skiereiland**	[skir·æjlant]
archipelago	**argipel**	[arχipəl]
bay, cove	**baai**	[bãi]
harbor	**hawe**	[havə]
lagoon	**strandmeer**	[strand·meər]
cape	**kaap**	[kãp]

atoll	atol	[atol]
reef	rif	[rif]
coral	koraal	[korāl]
coral reef	koraalrif	[korāl·rif]
deep (adj)	diep	[dip]
depth (deep water)	diepte	[diptə]
abyss	afgrond	[afχront]
trench (e.g., Mariana ~)	trog	[troχ]
current (Ocean ~)	stroming	[stromiŋ]
to surround (bathe)	omring	[omriŋ]
shore	oewer	[uvər]
coast	kus	[kus]
flow (flood tide)	hoogwater	[hoəχ·vatər]
ebb (ebb tide)	laagwater	[lāχ·vatər]
shoal	sandbank	[sand·bank]
bottom (~ of the sea)	bodem	[bodem]
wave	golf	[χolf]
crest (~ of a wave)	kruin	[krœin]
spume (sea foam)	skuim	[skœim]
storm (sea storm)	storm	[storm]
hurricane	orkaan	[orkān]
tsunami	tsunami	[tsunami]
calm (dead ~)	windstilte	[vindstiltə]
quiet, calm (adj)	kalm	[kalm]
pole	pool	[poəl]
polar (adj)	polêr	[polær]
latitude	breedtegraad	[breədtə·χrāt]
longitude	lengtegraad	[leŋtə·χrāt]
parallel	parallel	[parallel]
equator	ewenaar	[ɛvenār]
sky	hemel	[heməl]
horizon	horison	[horison]
air	lug	[luχ]
lighthouse	vuurtoring	[fɪrtoriŋ]
to dive (vi)	duik	[dœik]
to sink (ab. boat)	sink	[sink]
treasures	skatte	[skattə]

168. Mountains

mountain	berg	[berχ]
mountain range	bergreeks	[berχ·reəks]

mountain ridge	**bergrug**	[berχ·ruχ]
summit, top	**top**	[top]
peak	**piek**	[pik]
foot (~ of the mountain)	**voet**	[fut]
slope (mountainside)	**helling**	[hɛlliŋ]
volcano	**vulkaan**	[fulkān]
active volcano	**aktiewe vulkaan**	[aktivə fulkān]
dormant volcano	**rustende vulkaan**	[rustendə fulkān]
eruption	**uitbarsting**	[œitbarstiŋ]
crater	**krater**	[kratər]
magma	**magma**	[maχma]
lava	**lawa**	[lava]
molten (~ lava)	**gloeiende**	[χlujendə]
canyon	**diepkloof**	[dip·kloəf]
gorge	**kloof**	[kloəf]
crevice	**skeur**	[skøər]
abyss (chasm)	**afgrond**	[afχront]
pass, col	**bergpas**	[berχ·pas]
plateau	**plato**	[plato]
cliff	**krans**	[kraŋs]
hill	**kop**	[kop]
glacier	**gletser**	[χletsər]
waterfall	**waterval**	[vatər·fal]
geyser	**geiser**	[χæjsər]
lake	**meer**	[meər]
plain	**vlakte**	[flaktə]
landscape	**landskap**	[landskap]
echo	**eggo**	[ɛχχo]
alpinist	**alpinis**	[alpinis]
rock climber	**bergklimmer**	[berχ·klimmər]
to conquer (in climbing)	**baasraak**	[bāsrāk]
climb (an easy ~)	**beklimming**	[beklimmiŋ]

169. Rivers

river	**rivier**	[rifir]
spring (natural source)	**bron**	[bron]
riverbed (river channel)	**rivierbed**	[rifir·bet]
basin (river valley)	**stroomgebied**	[stroəm·χebit]
to flow into ...	**uitmond in ...**	[œitmont in …]
tributary	**syrivier**	[saj·rifir]
bank (of river)	**oewer**	[uvər]

current (stream)	stroming	[stromiŋ]
downstream (adv)	stroomafwaarts	[stroəm·afvārts]
upstream (adv)	stroomopwaarts	[stroəm·opvārts]

inundation	oorstroming	[oərstromiŋ]
flooding	oorstroming	[oərstromiŋ]
to overflow (vi)	oor sy walle loop	[oər saj vallə loəp]
to flood (vt)	oorstroom	[oərstroəm]

| shallow (shoal) | sandbank | [sand·bank] |
| rapids | stroomversnellings | [stroəm·fersnɛlliŋs] |

dam	damwal	[dam·wal]
canal	kanaal	[kanāl]
reservoir (artificial lake)	opgaardam	[opχār·dam]
sluice, lock	sluis	[slœis]

water body (pond, etc.)	dam	[dam]
swamp (marshland)	moeras	[muras]
bog, marsh	vlei	[flæj]
whirlpool	draaikolk	[drāj·kolk]

stream (brook)	spruit	[sprœit]
drinking (ab. water)	drink-	[drink-]
fresh (~ water)	vars	[fars]

ice	ys	[ajs]
to freeze over	bevries	[befris]
(ab. river, etc.)		

170. Forest

| forest, wood | bos | [bos] |
| forest (as adj) | bos- | [bos-] |

thick forest	woud	[væut]
grove	boord	[boərt]
forest clearing	oopte	[oəptə]

| thicket | struikgewas | [strœik·χevas] |
| scrubland | struikveld | [strœik·fɛlt] |

| footpath (troddenpath) | paadjie | [pādʒi] |
| gully | donga | [donχa] |

tree	boom	[boəm]
leaf	blaar	[blār]
leaves (foliage)	blare	[blarə]
fall of leaves	val van die blare	[fal fan di blarə]
to fall (ab. leaves)	val	[fal]

top (of the tree)	**boomtop**	[boəm·top]
branch	**tak**	[tak]
bough	**tak**	[tak]
bud (on shrub, tree)	**knop**	[knop]
needle (of pine tree)	**naald**	[nālt]
pine cone	**dennebol**	[dɛnnə·bol]
hollow (in a tree)	**holte**	[holtə]
nest	**nes**	[nes]
burrow (animal hole)	**gat**	[χat]
trunk	**stam**	[stam]
root	**wortel**	[vortəl]
bark	**bas**	[bas]
moss	**mos**	[mos]
to uproot (remove trees or tree stumps)	**ontwortel**	[ontwortəl]
to chop down	**omkap**	[omkap]
to deforest (vt)	**ontbos**	[ontbos]
tree stump	**boomstomp**	[boəm·stomp]
campfire	**kampvuur**	[kampfɪr]
forest fire	**bosbrand**	[bos·brant]
to extinguish (vt)	**blus**	[blus]
forest ranger	**boswagter**	[bos·waχtər]
protection	**beskerming**	[beskermiŋ]
to protect (~ nature)	**beskerm**	[beskerm]
poacher	**wildstroper**	[vilt·stropər]
steel trap	**slagyster**	[slaχ·ajstər]
to gather, to pick (vt)	**pluk**	[pluk]
to lose one's way	**verdwaal**	[ferdwāl]

171. Natural resources

natural resources	**natuurlike bronne**	[natɪrlikə bronnə]
minerals	**minerale**	[mineralə]
deposits	**lae**	[laə]
field (e.g., oilfield)	**veld**	[fɛlt]
to mine (extract)	**myn**	[majn]
mining (extraction)	**myn**	[majn]
ore	**erts**	[ɛrts]
mine (e.g., for coal)	**myn**	[majn]
shaft (mine ~)	**mynskag**	[majn·skaχ]
miner	**mynwerker**	[majn·werkər]
gas (natural ~)	**gas**	[χas]
gas pipeline	**gaspyp**	[χas·pajp]

oil (petroleum)	olie	[oli]
oil pipeline	olipypleiding	[oli·pajp·læjdiŋ]
oil well	oliebron	[oli·bron]
derrick (tower)	boortoring	[boər·toriŋ]
tanker	tenkskip	[tɛnk·skip]

sand	sand	[sant]
limestone	kalksteen	[kalksteən]
gravel	gruis	[xrœis]
peat	veengrond	[feənxront]
clay	klei	[klæj]
coal	steenkool	[steən·koəl]

iron (ore)	yster	[ajstər]
gold	goud	[xæʊt]
silver	silwer	[silwər]
nickel	nikkel	[nikkəl]
copper	koper	[kopər]

zinc	sink	[sink]
manganese	mangaan	[manxãn]
mercury	kwik	[kwik]
lead	lood	[loət]

mineral	mineraal	[minerãl]
crystal	kristal	[kristal]
marble	marmer	[marmər]
uranium	uraan	[urãn]

The Earth. Part 2

172. Weather

weather	weer	[veər]
weather forecast	weersvoorspelling	[veərs·foərspɛlliŋ]
temperature	temperatuur	[temperatɪr]
thermometer	termometer	[termometər]
barometer	barometer	[barometər]
humid (adj)	klam	[klam]
humidity	vogtigheid	[foχtiχæjt]
heat (extreme ~)	hitte	[hittə]
hot (torrid)	heet	[heət]
it's hot	dis vrekwarm	[dis frekvarm]
it's warm	dit is warm	[dit is varm]
warm (moderately hot)	louwarm	[læʊvarm]
it's cold	dis koud	[dis kæʊt]
cold (adj)	koud	[kæʊt]
sun	son	[son]
to shine (vi)	skyn	[skajn]
sunny (day)	sonnig	[sonnəχ]
to come up (vi)	opkom	[opkom]
to set (vi)	ondergaan	[ondərχān]
cloud	wolk	[volk]
cloudy (adj)	bewolk	[bevolk]
rain cloud	reënwolk	[reɛn·wolk]
somber (gloomy)	somber	[sombər]
rain	reën	[reɛn]
it's raining	dit reën	[dit reɛn]
rainy (~ day, weather)	reënerig	[reɛnerəχ]
to drizzle (vi)	motreën	[motreɛn]
pouring rain	stortbui	[stortbœi]
downpour	reënvlaag	[reɛn·flāχ]
heavy (e.g., ~ rain)	swaar	[swār]
puddle	poeletjie	[puləki]
to get wet (in rain)	nat word	[nat vort]
fog (mist)	mis	[mis]
foggy	mistig	[mistəχ]

| snow | sneeu | [sniʊ] |
| it's snowing | dit sneeu | [dit sniʊ] |

173. Severe weather. Natural disasters

thunderstorm	donderstorm	[dondər·storm]
lightning (~ strike)	weerlig	[veərləχ]
to flash (vi)	flits	[flits]

thunder	donder	[dondər]
to thunder (vi)	donder	[dondər]
it's thundering	dit donder	[dit dondər]

| hail | hael | [haəl] |
| it's hailing | dit hael | [dit haəl] |

| to flood (vt) | oorstroom | [oərstroəm] |
| flood, inundation | oorstroming | [oərstromiŋ] |

earthquake	aardbewing	[ārd·beviŋ]
tremor, quake	aardskok	[ārd·skok]
epicenter	episentrum	[ɛpisentrum]

| eruption | uitbarsting | [œitbarstiŋ] |
| lava | lawa | [lava] |

| twister, tornado | tornado | [tornado] |
| typhoon | tifoon | [tifoən] |

hurricane	orkaan	[orkān]
storm	storm	[storm]
tsunami	tsunami	[tsunami]

cyclone	sikloon	[sikloən]
bad weather	slegte weer	[sleχtə veər]
fire (accident)	brand	[brant]
disaster	ramp	[ramp]
meteorite	meteoriet	[meteorit]

avalanche	lawine	[lavinə]
snowslide	sneeulawine	[sniʊ·lavinə]
blizzard	sneeustorm	[sniʊ·storm]
snowstorm	sneeustorm	[sniʊ·storm]

Fauna

174. Mammals. Predators

predator	**roofdier**	[roəf·dir]
tiger	**tier**	[tir]
lion	**leeu**	[liʊ]
wolf	**wolf**	[volf]
fox	**vos**	[fos]
jaguar	**jaguar**	[jaχuar]
leopard	**luiperd**	[lœipert]
cheetah	**jagluiperd**	[jaχ·lœipert]
black panther	**swart luiperd**	[swart lœipert]
puma	**poema**	[puma]
snow leopard	**sneeuluiperd**	[sniʊ·lœipert]
lynx	**los**	[los]
coyote	**prêriewolf**	[præri·volf]
jackal	**jakkals**	[jakkals]
hyena	**hiëna**	[hiɛna]

175. Wild animals

animal	**dier**	[dir]
beast (animal)	**beest**	[beəst]
squirrel	**eekhoring**	[eəkhoriŋ]
hedgehog	**krimpvarkie**	[krimpfarki]
hare	**hasie**	[hasi]
rabbit	**konyn**	[konajn]
badger	**das**	[das]
raccoon	**wasbeer**	[vasbeər]
hamster	**hamster**	[hamstər]
marmot	**marmot**	[marmot]
mole	**mol**	[mol]
mouse	**muis**	[mœis]
rat	**rot**	[rot]
bat	**vlermuis**	[fler·mœis]
ermine	**hermelyn**	[herməlajn]
sable	**sabel, sabeldier**	[sabəl], [sabəl·dir]

marten	marter	[martər]
weasel	wesel	[vesəl]
mink	nerts	[nerts]

| beaver | bewer | [bevər] |
| otter | otter | [ottər] |

horse	perd	[pert]
moose	eland	[ɛlant]
deer	hert	[hert]
camel	kameel	[kameəl]

bison	bison	[bison]
aurochs	wisent	[visent]
buffalo	buffel	[buffəl]

zebra	sebra, kwagga	[sebra], [kwaχχa]
antelope	wildsbok	[vilds·bok]
roe deer	reebok	[reəbok]
fallow deer	damhert	[damhert]
chamois	gems	[χems]
wild boar	wildevark	[vildə·fark]

whale	walvis	[valfis]
seal	seehond	[seə·hont]
walrus	walrus	[valrus]
fur seal	seebeer	[seə·beər]
dolphin	dolfyn	[dolfajn]

bear	beer	[beər]
polar bear	ysbeer	[ajs·beər]
panda	panda	[panda]

monkey	aap	[āp]
chimpanzee	sjimpansee	[ʃimpaŋseə]
orangutan	orangoetang	[oranχutaŋ]
gorilla	gorilla	[χorilla]
macaque	makaak	[makāk]
gibbon	gibbon	[χibbon]

elephant	olifant	[olifant]
rhinoceros	renoster	[renostər]
giraffe	kameelperd	[kameəl·pert]
hippopotamus	seekoei	[seə·kui]

| kangaroo | kangaroe | [kanχaru] |
| koala (bear) | koala | [koala] |

mongoose	muishond	[mœis·hont]
chinchilla	chinchilla, tjintjilla	[tʃin·tʃila]
skunk	stinkmuishond	[stinkmœis·hont]
porcupine	ystervark	[ajstər·fark]

176. Domestic animals

cat	**kat**	[kat]
tomcat	**kater**	[katər]
dog	**hond**	[hont]
horse	**perd**	[pert]
stallion (male horse)	**hings**	[hiŋs]
mare	**merrie**	[merri]
cow	**koei**	[kui]
bull	**bul**	[bul]
ox	**os**	[os]
sheep (ewe)	**skaap**	[skãp]
ram	**ram**	[ram]
goat	**bok**	[bok]
billy goat, he-goat	**bokram**	[bok·ram]
donkey	**donkie, esel**	[donki], [eisəl]
mule	**muil**	[mœil]
pig, hog	**vark**	[fark]
piglet	**varkie**	[farki]
rabbit	**konyn**	[konajn]
hen (chicken)	**hoender, hen**	[hundər], [hen]
rooster	**haan**	[hãn]
duck	**eend**	[eent]
drake	**mannetjieseend**	[mannəkis·eent]
goose	**gans**	[χaŋs]
tom turkey, gobbler	**kalkoenmannetjie**	[kalkun·mannəki]
turkey (hen)	**kalkoen**	[kalkun]
domestic animals	**huisdiere**	[hœis·dirə]
tame (e.g., ~ hamster)	**mak**	[mak]
to tame (vt)	**mak maak**	[mak mãk]
to breed (vt)	**teel**	[teəl]
farm	**plaas**	[plãs]
poultry	**pluimvee**	[plœimfeə]
cattle	**beeste**	[beəstə]
herd (cattle)	**kudde**	[kuddə]
stable	**stal**	[stal]
pigpen	**varkstal**	[fark·stal]
cowshed	**koeistal**	[kui·stal]
rabbit hutch	**konynehok**	[konajne·hok]
hen house	**hoenderhok**	[hundər·hok]

177. Dogs. Dog breeds

dog	**hond**	[hont]
sheepdog	**herdershond**	[herdərs·hont]
German shepherd	**Duitse herdershond**	[dœitsə herdərs·hont]
poodle	**poedel**	[pudəl]
dachshund	**worshond**	[vors·hont]
bulldog	**bulhond**	[bul·hont]
boxer	**bokser**	[boksər]
mastiff	**mastiff**	[mastif]
Rottweiler	**Rottweiler**	[rottwæjlər]
Doberman	**Dobermann**	[dobermann]
basset	**basset**	[basset]
bobtail	**bobtail**	[bobtajl]
Dalmatian	**Dalmatiese hond**	[dalmatisə hont]
cocker spaniel	**sniphond**	[snip·hont]
Newfoundland	**Newfoundlander**	[njufæʊntlandər]
Saint Bernard	**Sint Bernard**	[sint bernart]
husky	**poolhond, husky**	[pulhont], [huski]
Chow Chow	**chowchow**	[tʃau·tʃau]
spitz	**spitshond**	[spits·hont]
pug	**mopshond**	[mops·hont]

178. Sounds made by animals

barking (n)	**geblaf**	[χeblaf]
to bark (vi)	**blaf**	[blaf]
to meow (vi)	**miaau**	[miãu]
to purr (vi)	**spin**	[spin]
to moo (vi)	**loei**	[lui]
to bellow (bull)	**bulk**	[bulk]
to growl (vi)	**grom**	[χrom]
howl (n)	**gehuil**	[χehœil]
to howl (vi)	**huil**	[hœil]
to whine (vi)	**tjank**	[tʃank]
to bleat (sheep)	**blêr**	[blær]
to oink, to grunt (pig)	**snork**	[snork]
to squeal (vi)	**gil**	[χil]
to croak (vi)	**kwaak**	[kwãk]
to buzz (insect)	**zoem**	[zum]
to chirp (crickets, grasshopper)	**kriek**	[krik]

179. Birds

bird	voël	[foɛl]
pigeon	duif	[dœif]
sparrow	mossie	[mossi]
tit (great tit)	mees	[meəs]
magpie	ekster	[ɛkstər]

raven	raaf	[rãf]
crow	kraai	[krãi]
jackdaw	kerkkraai	[kerk·krãi]
rook	roek	[ruk]

duck	eend	[eent]
goose	gans	[χaŋs]
pheasant	fisant	[fisant]

eagle	arend	[arɛnt]
hawk	sperwer	[sperwər]
falcon	valk	[falk]
vulture	aasvoël	[ãsfoɛl]
condor (Andean ~)	kondor	[kondor]

swan	swaan	[swãn]
crane	kraanvoël	[krãn·foɛl]
stork	ooievaar	[ojefãr]

parrot	papegaai	[papəχãi]
hummingbird	kolibrie	[kolibri]
peacock	pou	[pæʊ]

ostrich	volstruis	[folstrœis]
heron	reier	[ræjer]
flamingo	flamink	[flamink]
pelican	pelikaan	[pelikãn]

nightingale	nagtegaal	[naχteχãl]
swallow	swael	[swaəl]

thrush	lyster	[lajstər]
song thrush	sanglyster	[saŋlajstər]
blackbird	merel	[merəl]

swift	windswael	[vindswaəl]
lark	lewerik	[leverik]
quail	kwartel	[kwartəl]

woodpecker	speg	[speχ]
cuckoo	koekoek	[kukuk]
owl	uil	[œil]
eagle owl	ooruil	[oərœil]

wood grouse	**auerhoen**	[ɔuer·hun]
black grouse	**korhoen**	[korhun]
partridge	**patrys**	[patrajs]

starling	**spreeu**	[spriʋ]
canary	**kanarie**	[kanari]
hazel grouse	**bonasa hoen**	[bonasa hun]
chaffinch	**gryskoppie**	[χrajskoppi]
bullfinch	**bloedvink**	[bludfink]

seagull	**seemeeu**	[seəmiʋ]
albatross	**albatros**	[albatros]
penguin	**pikkewyn**	[pikkəvajn]

180. Birds. Singing and sounds

to sing (vi)	**fluit**	[flœit]
to call (animal, bird)	**roep**	[rup]
to crow (rooster)	**kraai**	[krãi]
cock-a-doodle-doo	**koekelekoe**	[kukeleku]

to cluck (hen)	**kekkel**	[kɛkkəl]
to caw (vi)	**kras**	[kras]
to quack (duck)	**kwaak**	[kwãk]
to cheep (vi)	**piep**	[pip]
to chirp, to twitter	**tjilp**	[tʃilp]

181. Fish. Marine animals

| bream | **brasem** | [brasem] |
| carp | **karp** | [karp] |

perch	**baars**	[bãrs]
catfish	**katvis, seebaber**	[katfis], [see·babər]
pike	**snoek**	[snuk]

| salmon | **salm** | [salm] |
| sturgeon | **steur** | [støər] |

herring	**haring**	[hariŋ]
Atlantic salmon	**atlantiese salm**	[atlantisə salm]
mackerel	**makriel**	[makril]
flatfish	**platvis**	[platfis]

zander, pike perch	**varswatersnoek**	[farswatər·snuk]
cod	**kabeljou**	[kabeljæʋ]
tuna	**tuna**	[tuna]
trout	**forel**	[forəl]

eel	paling	[paliŋ]
electric ray	drilvis	[drilfis]
moray eel	bontpaling	[bontpaliŋ]
piranha	piranha	[piranha]

shark	haai	[hāi]
dolphin	dolfyn	[dolfajn]
whale	walvis	[valfis]

crab	krap	[krap]
jellyfish	jellievis	[jelli·fis]
octopus	seekat	[seə·kat]

starfish	seester	[seə·stər]
sea urchin	see-egel, seekastaiing	[seə-eχel], [seə·kastajiŋ]
seahorse	seeperdjie	[seə·perʤi]

oyster	oester	[ustər]
shrimp	garnaal	[χarnāl]
lobster	kreef	[kreəf]
spiny lobster	seekreef	[seə·kreəf]

182. Amphibians. Reptiles

snake	slang	[slaŋ]
venomous (snake)	giftig	[χiftəχ]

viper	adder	[addər]
cobra	kobra	[kobra]

python	luislang	[lœislaŋ]
boa	boa, konstriktorslang	[boa], [kɔŋstriktor·slaŋ]

grass snake	ringslang	[riŋ·slaŋ]
rattle snake	ratelslang	[ratəl·slaŋ]
anaconda	anakonda	[anakonda]

lizard	akkedis	[akkedis]
iguana	leguaan	[leχuān]
monitor lizard	likkewaan	[likkevān]
salamander	salamander	[salamandər]

chameleon	verkleurmannetjie	[ferkløər·manneki]
scorpion	skerpioen	[skerpiun]

turtle	skilpad	[skilpat]
frog	padda	[padda]

toad	brulpadda	[brul·padda]
crocodile	krokodil	[krokodil]

183. Insects

insect, bug	insek	[insek]
butterfly	skoenlapper	[skunlappər]
ant	mier	[mir]
fly	vlieg	[fliχ]
mosquito	muskiet	[muskit]
beetle	kewer	[kevər]
wasp	perdeby	[perdə·baj]
bee	by	[baj]
bumblebee	hommelby	[hommel·baj]
gadfly (botfly)	perdevlieg	[perdə·fliχ]
spider	spinnekop	[spinnə·kop]
spiderweb	spinnerak	[spinnə·rak]
dragonfly	naaldekoker	[näldə·kokər]
grasshopper	sprinkaan	[sprinkän]
moth (night butterfly)	mot	[mot]
cockroach	kakkerlak	[kakkerlak]
tick	bosluis	[boslœis]
flea	vlooi	[floj]
midge	muggie	[muχχi]
locust	treksprinkhaan	[trek·sprinkhän]
snail	slak	[slak]
cricket	kriek	[krik]
lightning bug	vuurvliegie	[fɪrfliχi]
ladybug	lieweheersbesie	[liveheərs·besi]
cockchafer	lentekewer	[lentekevər]
leech	bloedsuier	[blud·sœiər]
caterpillar	ruspe	[ruspə]
earthworm	erdwurm	[ɛrd·vurm]
larva	larwe	[larvə]

184. Animals. Body parts

beak	snawel	[snavəl]
wings	vlerke	[flerkə]
foot (of bird)	poot	[poət]
feathers (plumage)	vere	[ferə]
feather	veer	[feər]
crest	kuif	[kœif]
gills	kiewe	[kivə]
spawn	viseiers	[fisæjers]

larva	**larwe**	[larvə]
fin	**vin**	[fin]
scales (of fish, reptile)	**skubbe**	[skubbə]
fang (canine)	**slagtand**	[slaχtant]
paw (e.g., cat's ~)	**poot**	[poət]
muzzle (snout)	**muil**	[mœil]
mouth (of cat, dog)	**bek**	[bek]
tail	**stert**	[stert]
whiskers	**snor**	[snor]
hoof	**hoef**	[huf]
horn	**horing**	[horiŋ]
carapace	**rugdop**	[ruχdop]
shell (of mollusk)	**skulp**	[skulp]
eggshell	**eierdop**	[æjer·dop]
animal's hair (pelage)	**pels**	[pɛls]
pelt (hide)	**vel**	[fəl]

185. Animals. Habitats

habitat	**habitat**	[habitat]
migration	**migrasie**	[miχrasi]
mountain	**berg**	[berχ]
reef	**rif**	[rif]
cliff	**rots**	[rots]
forest	**woud**	[væʊt]
jungle	**oerwoud**	[urwæʊt]
savanna	**veld**	[fɛlt]
tundra	**toendra**	[tundra]
steppe	**steppe**	[stɛppə]
desert	**woestyn**	[vustajn]
oasis	**oase**	[oasə]
sea	**see**	[seə]
lake	**meer**	[meər]
ocean	**oseaan**	[oseān]
swamp (marshland)	**moeras**	[muras]
freshwater (adj)	**varswater**	[fars·vatər]
pond	**dam**	[dam]
river	**rivier**	[rifir]
den (bear's ~)	**hol**	[hol]
nest	**nes**	[nes]

hollow (in a tree)	**holte**	[holtə]
burrow (animal hole)	**gat**	[χat]
anthill	**miershoop**	[mirs·hoəp]

Flora

186. Trees

tree	**boom**	[boəm]
deciduous (adj)	**bladwisselend**	[bladwisselent]
coniferous (adj)	**kegeldraend**	[keχεldraent]
evergreen (adj)	**immergroen**	[immərχrun]
apple tree	**appelboom**	[appεl·boəm]
pear tree	**peerboom**	[peər·boəm]
cherry tree	**kersieboom**	[kersi·boəm]
sweet cherry tree	**soetkersieboom**	[sutkersi·boəm]
sour cherry tree	**suurkersieboom**	[sɪrkersi·boəm]
plum tree	**pruimeboom**	[prœimə·boəm]
birch	**berk**	[berk]
oak	**eik**	[æjk]
linden tree	**lindeboom**	[lində·boəm]
aspen	**trilpopulier**	[trilpopulir]
maple	**esdoring**	[εsdoriŋ]
spruce	**spar**	[spar]
pine	**denneboom**	[dεnnə·boəm]
larch	**lorkeboom**	[lorkə·boəm]
fir tree	**den**	[den]
cedar	**seder**	[sedər]
poplar	**populier**	[populir]
rowan	**lysterbessie**	[lajstərbεssi]
willow	**wilger**	[vilχər]
alder	**els**	[εls]
beech	**beuk**	[bøək]
elm	**olm**	[olm]
ash (tree)	**esboom**	[εs·boəm]
chestnut	**kastaiing**	[kastajiŋ]
magnolia	**magnolia**	[maχnolia]
palm tree	**palm**	[palm]
cypress	**sipres**	[sipres]
mangrove	**wortelboom**	[vortəl·boəm]
baobab	**kremetart**	[kremetart]
eucalyptus	**bloekom**	[blukom]
sequoia	**mammoetboom**	[mammut·boəm]

187. Shrubs

| bush | struik | [strœik] |
| shrub | bossie | [bossi] |

| grapevine | wingerdstok | [viŋərd·stok] |
| vineyard | wingerd | [viŋərt] |

raspberry bush	framboosstruik	[framboəs·strœik]
blackcurrant bush	swartbessiestruik	[swartbɛssi·strœik]
redcurrant bush	rooi aalbessiestruik	[roj ālbɛssi·strœik]
gooseberry bush	appelliefiestruik	[appɛllifi·strœik]

acacia	akasia	[akasia]
barberry	suurbessie	[sɪr·bɛssi]
jasmine	jasmyn	[jasmajn]

juniper	jenewer	[jenevər]
rosebush	roosstruik	[roəs·strœik]
dog rose	hondsroos	[honds·roəs]

188. Mushrooms

mushroom	paddastoel	[paddastul]
edible mushroom	eetbare paddastoel	[eetbarə paddastul]
poisonous mushroom	giftige paddastoel	[χiftiχə paddastul]
cap (of mushroom)	hoed	[hut]
stipe (of mushroom)	steel	[steəl]

cep (Boletus edulis)	Eetbare boleet	[eetbarə boleət]
orange-cap boletus	rooihoed	[rojhut]
birch bolete	berkboleet	[berk·boleət]
chanterelle	dooierswam	[dojer·swam]
russula	russula	[russula]

morel	morielje	[morilje]
fly agaric	vlieëswam	[fliɛ·swam]
death cap	duiwelsbrood	[dœivɛls·broət]

189. Fruits. Berries

| fruit | vrug | [fruχ] |
| fruits | vrugte | [fruχtə] |

apple	appel	[appəl]
pear	peer	[peər]
plum	pruim	[prœim]

strawberry (garden ~)	aarbei	[ārbæj]
cherry	kersie	[kersi]
sour cherry	suurkersie	[sɪr·kersi]
sweet cherry	soetkersie	[sut·kersi]
grape	druif	[drœif]
raspberry	framboos	[framboəs]
blackcurrant	swartbessie	[swartbɛssi]
redcurrant	rooi aalbessie	[roj ālbɛssi]
gooseberry	appelliefie	[appɛllifi]
cranberry	bosbessie	[bosbɛssi]
orange	lemoen	[lemun]
mandarin	nartjie	[narki]
pineapple	pynappel	[pajnappəl]
banana	piesang	[pisaŋ]
date	dadel	[dadəl]
lemon	suurlemoen	[sɪr·lemun]
apricot	appelkoos	[appɛlkoəs]
peach	perske	[perskə]
kiwi	kiwi, kiwivrug	[kivi], [kivi·fruχ]
grapefruit	pomelo	[pomelo]
berry	bessie	[bɛssi]
berries	bessies	[bɛssis]
cowberry	pryselbessie	[prajsɛlbɛssi]
wild strawberry	wilde aarbei	[vildə ārbæj]
bilberry	bloubessie	[blæubɛssi]

190. Flowers. Plants

flower	blom	[blom]
bouquet (of flowers)	boeket	[buket]
rose (flower)	roos	[roəs]
tulip	tulp	[tulp]
carnation	angelier	[anχəlir]
gladiolus	swaardlelie	[swārd·leli]
cornflower	koringblom	[koriŋblom]
harebell	grasklokkie	[χras·klokki]
dandelion	perdeblom	[perdə·blom]
camomile	kamille	[kamillə]
aloe	aalwyn	[ālwajn]
cactus	kaktus	[kaktus]
rubber plant, ficus	rubberplant	[rubbər·plant]
lily	lelie	[leli]
geranium	malva	[mɑlfa]

hyacinth	**hiasint**	[hiasint]
mimosa	**mimosa**	[mimosa]
narcissus	**narsing**	[narsiŋ]
nasturtium	**kappertjie**	[kapperki]
orchid	**orgidee**	[orχideə]
peony	**pinksterroos**	[pinkstər·roəs]
violet	**viooltjie**	[fioəlki]
pansy	**gesiggie**	[χesiχi]
forget-me-not	**vergeet-my-nietjie**	[ferχeət-maj-niki]
daisy	**madeliefie**	[madelifi]
poppy	**papawer**	[papavər]
hemp	**hennep**	[hɛnnəp]
mint	**kruisement**	[krœisəment]
lily of the valley	**dallelie**	[dalleli]
snowdrop	**sneeuklokkie**	[sniʊ·klokki]
nettle	**brandnetel**	[brant·netəl]
sorrel	**veldsuring**	[fɛltsuriŋ]
water lily	**waterlelie**	[vatər·leli]
fern	**varing**	[fariŋ]
lichen	**korsmos**	[korsmos]
greenhouse (tropical ~)	**broeikas**	[bruikas]
lawn	**grasperk**	[χras·perk]
flowerbed	**blombed**	[blom·bet]
plant	**plant**	[plant]
grass	**gras**	[χras]
blade of grass	**grasspriet**	[χras·sprit]
leaf	**blaar**	[blãr]
petal	**kroonblaar**	[kroən·blãr]
stem	**stingel**	[stiŋəl]
tuber	**knol**	[knol]
young plant (shoot)	**saailing**	[sãjliŋ]
thorn	**doring**	[doriŋ]
to blossom (vi)	**bloei**	[blui]
to fade, to wither	**verlep**	[ferlep]
smell (odor)	**reuk**	[røək]
to cut (flowers)	**sny**	[snaj]
to pick (a flower)	**pluk**	[pluk]

191. Cereals, grains

grain	**graan**	[χrãn]
cereal crops	**graangewasse**	[χrãn·χəwassə]

ear (of barley, etc.)	**aar**	[ār]
wheat	**koring**	[koriŋ]
rye	**rog**	[roχ]
oats	**hawer**	[havər]
millet	**gierst**	[χirst]
barley	**gars**	[χars]
corn	**mielie**	[mili]
rice	**rys**	[rajs]
buckwheat	**bokwiet**	[bokwit]
pea plant	**ertjie**	[ɛrki]
kidney bean	**nierboon**	[nir·boən]
soy	**soja**	[soja]
lentil	**lensie**	[lɛŋsi]
beans (pulse crops)	**boontjies**	[boənkis]

REGIONAL GEOGRAPHY

Countries. Nationalities

192. Politics. Government. Part 1

politics	politiek	[politik]
political (adj)	politieke	[politikə]
politician	politikus	[politikus]
state (country)	staat	[stāt]
citizen	burger	[burgər]
citizenship	burgerskap	[burgərskap]
national emblem	nasionale wapen	[naʃionalə vapen]
national anthem	volkslied	[folkslit]
government	regering	[reꭓeriŋ]
head of state	staatshoof	[stāts·hoəf]
parliament	parlement	[parlement]
party	partij	[partij]
capitalism	kapitalisme	[kapitalismə]
capitalist (adj)	kapitalis	[kapitalis]
socialism	sosialisme	[soʃialismə]
socialist (adj)	sosialis	[soʃialis]
communism	kommunisme	[kommunismə]
communist (adj)	kommunis	[kommunis]
communist (n)	kommunis	[kommunis]
democracy	demokrasie	[demokrasi]
democrat	demokraat	[demokrāt]
democratic (adj)	demokraties	[demokratis]
Democratic party	Demokratiese party	[demokratisə partaj]
liberal (n)	liberaal	[liberāl]
liberal (adj)	liberaal	[liberāl]
conservative (n)	konservatief	[koŋserfatif]
conservative (adj)	konservatief	[koŋserfatif]
republic (n)	republiek	[republik]
republican (n)	republikein	[republikæjn]

Republican party	**Republikeinse Party**	[republikæjnsə partaj]
elections	**verkiesings**	[ferkisiŋs]
to elect (vt)	**verkies**	[ferkis]
elector, voter	**kieser**	[kisər]
election campaign	**verkiesingskampanje**	[ferkisiŋs·kampanje]
voting (n)	**stemming**	[stɛmmiŋ]
to vote (vi)	**stem**	[stem]
suffrage, right to vote	**stemreg**	[stem·reχ]
candidate	**kandidaat**	[kandidāt]
campaign	**kampanje**	[kampanje]
opposition (as adj)	**opposisie**	[opposisi]
opposition (n)	**opposisie**	[opposisi]
visit	**besoek**	[besuk]
official visit	**amptelike besoek**	[amptelikə besuk]
international (adj)	**internasionaal**	[internaʃionāl]
negotiations	**onderhandelinge**	[ondərhandeliŋə]
to negotiate (vi)	**onderhandel**	[ondərhandəl]

193. Politics. Government. Part 2

society	**samelewing**	[sameleviŋ]
constitution	**grondwet**	[χront·wet]
power (political control)	**mag**	[maχ]
corruption	**korrupsie**	[korrupsi]
law (justice)	**wet**	[vet]
legal (legitimate)	**wetlik**	[vetlik]
justice (fairness)	**geregtigheid**	[χereχtiχæjt]
just (fair)	**regverdig**	[reχferdəχ]
committee	**komitee**	[komiteə]
bill (draft law)	**wetsontwerp**	[vetsontwerp]
budget	**begroting**	[beχrotiŋ]
policy	**beleid**	[belæjt]
reform	**hervorming**	[herformiŋ]
radical (adj)	**radikaal**	[radikāl]
power (strength, force)	**mag**	[maχ]
powerful (adj)	**magtig**	[maχtəχ]
supporter	**ondersteuner**	[ondərstøənər]
influence	**invloed**	[influt]
regime (e.g., military ~)	**bewind**	[bevint]
conflict	**konflik**	[konflik]

| conspiracy (plot) | sameswering | [samesweriŋ] |
| provocation | uitdaging | [œitdaχiŋ] |

to overthrow (regime, etc.)	omvergooi	[omferχoj]
overthrow (of government)	omvergooi	[omferχoj]
revolution	revolusie	[refolusi]

| coup d'état | staatsgreep | [stāts·χreəp] |
| military coup | militère staatsgreep | [militærə stātsχreəp] |

crisis	krisis	[krisis]
economic recession	ekonomiese agteruitgang	[ɛkonomisə aχtər·œitχaŋ]
demonstrator (protester)	betoër	[betoɛr]
demonstration	demonstrasie	[demoŋstrasi]
martial law	krygswet	[krajχs·wet]
military base	militère basis	[militærə basis]

| stability | stabiliteit | [stabilitæjt] |
| stable (adj) | stabiel | [stabil] |

| exploitation | uitbuiting | [œitbœitiŋ] |
| to exploit (workers) | uitbuit | [œitbœit] |

racism	rassisme	[rassismə]
racist	rassis	[rassis]
fascism	fascisme	[faʃismə]
fascist	fascis	[faʃis]

194. Countries. Miscellaneous

foreigner	vreemdeling	[freəmdeliŋ]
foreign (adj)	vreemd	[freəmt]
abroad (in a foreign country)	in die buiteland	[in di bœitəlant]

emigrant	emigrant	[ɛmiχrant]
emigration	emigrasie	[ɛmiχrasi]
to emigrate (vi)	emigreer	[ɛmiχreər]

the West	die Weste	[di vestə]
the East	die Ooste	[di oəstə]
the Far East	die Verre Ooste	[di ferrə oəstə]

civilization	beskawing	[beskaviŋ]
humanity (mankind)	mensdom	[mɛŋsdom]
the world (earth)	die wèreld	[di værəlt]
peace	vrede	[fredə]
worldwide (adj)	wèreldwyd	[værəlt·wajt]
homeland	vaderland	[fadər·lant]

people (population)	volk	[folk]
population	bevolking	[befolkiŋ]
people (a lot of ~)	mense	[mɛŋsə]
nation (people)	nasie	[nasi]
generation	generasie	[χenerasi]

territory (area)	gebied	[χebit]
region	streek	[streək]
state (part of a country)	staat	[stãt]

tradition	tradisie	[tradisi]
custom (tradition)	gebruik	[χebrœik]
ecology	ekologie	[ɛkoloχi]

Indian (Native American)	Indiaan	[indiãn]
Gypsy (masc.)	Sigeuner	[siχøənər]
Gypsy (fem.)	Sigeunerin	[siχøənərin]
Gypsy (adj)	sigeuner-	[siχøənər-]

empire	rijk	[rijk]
colony	kolonie	[koloni]
slavery	slawerny	[slavərnaj]
invasion	invasie	[infasi]
famine	hongersnood	[hoŋərsnoət]

195. Major religious groups. Confessions

| religion | godsdiens | [χodsdiŋs] |
| religious (adj) | godsdienstig | [χodsdiŋstəχ] |

faith, belief	geloof	[χeloəf]
to believe (in God)	glo	[χlo]
believer	gelowige	[χeloviχə]

| atheism | ateïsme | [ateïsmə] |
| atheist | ateïs | [ateïs] |

Christianity	Christendom	[χristəndom]
Christian (n)	Christen	[χristən]
Christian (adj)	Christelik	[χristəlik]

Catholicism	Katolisisme	[katolisismə]
Catholic (n)	Katoliek	[katolik]
Catholic (adj)	katoliek	[katolik]

Protestantism	Protestantisme	[protestantismə]
Protestant Church	Protestantse Kerk	[protestantsə kerk]
Protestant (n)	Protestant	[protestant]
Orthodoxy	Ortodoksie	[ortodoksi]
Orthodox Church	Ortodokse Kerk	[ortodoksə kerk]

Orthodox (n)	Ortodoks	[ortodoks]
Presbyterianism	Presbiterianisme	[presbiterianismə]
Presbyterian Church	Presbiteriaanse Kerk	[presbiteriãŋsə kerk]
Presbyterian (n)	Presbiteriaan	[presbitəriãn]

| Lutheranism | Lutheranisme | [luteranismə] |
| Lutheran (n) | Lutheraan | [lutərãn] |

| Baptist Church | Baptistiese Kerk | [baptistisə kerk] |
| Baptist (n) | Baptis | [baptis] |

| Anglican Church | Anglikaanse Kerk | [anχlikãŋsə kerk] |
| Anglican (n) | Anglikaan | [anχlikãn] |

| Mormonism | Mormonisme | [mormonismə] |
| Mormon (n) | Mormoon | [mormoən] |

| Judaism | Jodendom | [jodɛndom] |
| Jew (n) | Jood | [joət] |

| Buddhism | Boeddhisme | [buddismə] |
| Buddhist (n) | Boeddhis | [buddis] |

| Hinduism | Hindoeïsme | [hinduïsmə] |
| Hindu (n) | Hindoe | [hindu] |

Islam	Islam	[islam]
Muslim (n)	Islamiet	[islamit]
Muslim (adj)	Islamities	[islamitis]

| Shiah Islam | Sjia Islam | [ʃia islam] |
| Shiite (n) | Sjiit | [ʃiit] |

| Sunni Islam | Sunni Islam | [sunni islam] |
| Sunnite (n) | Sunniet | [sunnit] |

196. Religions. Priests

| priest | priester | [pristər] |
| the Pope | die Pous | [di pæʊs] |

monk, friar	monnik	[monnik]
nun	non	[non]
pastor	pastoor	[pastoər]

abbot	ab	[ap]
vicar (parish priest)	priester	[pristər]
bishop	biskop	[biskop]
cardinal	kardinaal	[kardinãl]
preacher	predikant	[predikant]

| preaching | preek | [preek] |
| parishioners | kerkgangers | [kerk·xaŋers] |

| believer | gelowige | [xeloviχe] |
| atheist | ateïs | [ateïs] |

197. Faith. Christianity. Islam

| Adam | Adam | [adam] |
| Eve | Eva | [efa] |

God	God	[χot]
the Lord	die Here	[di here]
the Almighty	die Almagtige	[di almaχtiχe]

sin	sonde	[sonde]
to sin (vi)	sondig	[sondeχ]
sinner (masc.)	sondaar	[sondãr]
sinner (fem.)	sondares	[sondares]

| hell | hel | [hel] |
| paradise | paradys | [paradajs] |

| Jesus | Jesus | [jesus] |
| Jesus Christ | Jesus Christus | [jesus χristus] |

the Holy Spirit	die Heilige Gees	[di hæjliχe χees]
the Savior	die Verlosser	[di ferlosser]
the Virgin Mary	die Maagd Maria	[di mãχt maria]

the Devil	die duiwel	[di dœivel]
devil's (adj)	duiwels	[dœivɛls]
Satan	Satan	[satan]
satanic (adj)	satanies	[satanis]

angel	engel	[ɛŋel]
guardian angel	beskermengel	[beskerm·eŋel]
angelic (adj)	engelagtig	[ɛŋelaχteχ]

apostle	apostel	[apostel]
archangel	aartsengel	[ãrtseŋel]
the Antichrist	die antichris	[di antiχris]

Church	Kerk	[kerk]
Bible	Bybel	[bajbel]
biblical (adj)	bybels	[bajbels]

Old Testament	Ou Testament	[æʊ testament]
New Testament	Nuwe Testament	[nuve testament]
Gospel	evangelie	[ɛfanχeli]

| Holy Scripture | Heilige Skrif | [hæjliχə skrif] |
| Heaven | hemel | [heməl] |

Commandment	gebod	[χebot]
prophet	profeet	[profeət]
prophecy	profesie	[profesi]

Allah	Allah	[allah]
Mohammed	Mohammed	[mohammet]
the Koran	die Koran	[di koran]

mosque	moskee	[moskeə]
mullah	moella	[mulla]
prayer	gebed	[χebet]
to pray (vi, vt)	bid	[bit]

pilgrimage	pelgrimstog	[pɛlχrimstoχ]
pilgrim	pelgrim	[pɛlχrim]
Mecca	Mecca	[mɛkka]

church	kerk	[kerk]
temple	tempel	[tempəl]
cathedral	katedraal	[katedrãl]
Gothic (adj)	Goties	[χotis]
synagogue	sinagoge	[sinaχoχə]
mosque	moskee	[moskeə]

chapel	kapel	[kapəl]
abbey	abdy	[abdaj]
convent	klooster	[kloəstər]
monastery	klooster	[kloəstər]

bell (church ~s)	klok	[klok]
bell tower	kloktoring	[klok·toriŋ]
to ring (ab. bells)	lui	[lœi]

cross	kruis	[krœis]
cupola (roof)	koepel	[kupəl]
icon	ikoon	[ikoən]

soul	siel	[sil]
fate (destiny)	noodlot	[noədlot]
evil (n)	die bose	[di bosə]
good (n)	goed	[χut]

vampire	vampier	[fampir]
witch (evil ~)	heks	[heks]
demon	demoon	[demoən]
spirit	gees	[χeəs]

| redemption (giving us ~) | versoening | [fersuniŋ] |
| to redeem (vt) | verlos | [ferlos] |

church service, mass	kerkdies	[kerkdis]
to say mass	die mis opdra	[di mis opdra]
confession	bieg	[biχ]
to confess (vi)	bieg	[biχ]

saint (n)	heilige	[hæjliχə]
sacred (holy)	heilig	[hæjləχ]
holy water	wywater	[vaj·vatər]

ritual (n)	ritueel	[ritueəl]
ritual (adj)	ritueel	[ritueəl]
sacrifice	offerande	[offerandə]

superstition	bygeloof	[bajχəloəf]
superstitious (adj)	bygelowig	[bajχəlovəχ]
afterlife	hiernamaals	[hirna·māls]
eternal life	ewige lewe	[εviχə levə]

MISCELLANEOUS

198. Various useful words

background (green ~)	agtergrond	[aχtərχront]
balance (of situation)	balans	[balaŋs]
barrier (obstacle)	hindernis	[hindərnis]
base (basis)	basis	[basis]
beginning	begin	[beχin]
category	kategorie	[kateχori]
cause (reason)	rede	[redə]
choice	keuse	[køøsə]
coincidence	toeval	[tufal]
comfortable (~ chair)	gemaklik	[χemaklik]
comparison	vergelyking	[ferχelajkiŋ]
compensation	kompensasie	[kompɛnsasi]
degree (extent, amount)	graad	[χrãt]
development	ontwikkeling	[ontwikkeliŋ]
difference	verskil	[ferskil]
effect (e.g., of drugs)	effek	[ɛffek]
effort (exertion)	inspanning	[inspanniŋ]
element	element	[ɛlement]
end (finish)	einde	[æjndə]
example (illustration)	voorbeeld	[foərbeelt]
fact	feit	[fæjt]
frequent (adj)	gereeld	[χereelt]
growth (development)	groei	[χrui]
help	hulp	[hulp]
ideal	ideaal	[ideãl]
kind (sort, type)	soort	[soərt]
labyrinth	labirint	[labirint]
mistake, error	fout	[fæʊt]
moment	moment	[moment]
object (thing)	objek	[objek]
obstacle	hinderpaal	[hindərpãl]
original (original copy)	origineel	[oriχineel]
part (~ of sth)	deel	[deəl]
particle, small part	deeltjie	[deəlki]
pause (break)	pouse	[pæʊsə]

position	**posisie**	[posisi]
principle	**beginsel**	[beχinsəl]
problem	**probleem**	[probleəm]

process	**proses**	[proses]
progress	**vooruitgang**	[foərœitχaŋ]
property (quality)	**eienskap**	[æjeŋskap]

| reaction | **reaksie** | [reaksi] |
| risk | **risiko** | [risiko] |

secret	**geheim**	[χəhæjm]
series	**reeks**	[reəks]
shape (outer form)	**vorm**	[form]
situation	**toestand**	[tustant]
solution	**oplossing**	[oplossiŋ]

standard (adj)	**standaard**	[standãrt]
standard (level of quality)	**standaard**	[standãrt]
stop (pause)	**pouse**	[pæusə]
style	**styl**	[stajl]

system	**sisteem**	[sisteəm]
table (chart)	**tabel**	[tabəl]
tempo, rate	**tempo**	[tempo]
term (word, expression)	**term**	[term]

thing (object, item)	**ding**	[diŋ]
truth (e.g., moment of ~)	**waarheid**	[vãrhæjt]
turn (please wait your ~)	**beurt**	[bøørt]
type (sort, kind)	**tipe**	[tipə]
urgent (adj)	**dringend**	[driŋən]

urgently (adv)	**dringend**	[driŋən]
utility (usefulness)	**nut**	[nut]
variant (alternative)	**variant**	[fariant]
way (means, method)	**manier**	[manir]
zone	**sone**	[sonə]

* 9 7 8 1 7 8 7 1 6 4 8 4 0 *